Implementing Microsoft Dynamics AX 2012 with Sure Step 2012

Get to grips with AX 2012 and learn a whole host of tips and tricks to ensure project success

Keith Dunkinson

Andrew Birch

[PACKT] PUBLISHING enterprise
professional expertise distilled

BIRMINGHAM - MUMBAI

Implementing Microsoft Dynamics AX 2012 with Sure Step 2012

First published: March 2013

Production Reference: 1110313

Published by Packt Publishing Ltd.
Livery Place
35 Livery Street
Birmingham B3 2PB, UK.

ISBN 978-1-84968-704-1

www.packtpub.com

Cover Image by Abhishek Pandey (abhishek.pandey1210@gmail.com)

Credits

Authors
Keith Dunkinson
Andrew Birch

Reviewers
Simon Buxton
Marco A. Carvalho
Angela McClelland
David Probst
Mohammed Rasheed

Acquisition Editor
Mary Nadar

Lead Technical Editor
Ankita Shashi

Technical Editors
Worrell Lewis
Amit Ramadas

Project Coordinator
Leena Purkait

Proofreader
Mario Cecere

Indexers
Hemangini Bari
Tejal Soni

Graphics
Valentina D'Silva

Production Coordinator
Nilesh R. Mohite

Cover Work
Nilesh R. Mohite

About the Authors

Keith Dunkinson has over 20 years experience implementing ERP systems for a number of companies, taking part in over 100 successful ERP implementations. He owned and ran The Computing Practice, an ERP Solution Centre, where he worked in a variety of roles for over 16 years, selling and implementing Dynamics NAV, SAP, Oracle, and Sage software. Keith now works as the Business Development Director at AxPact Limited—the world's largest global supplier of Microsoft Dynamics AX, where he is involved in bringing together and managing over 30 independent Dynamics AX Solution Centers and leads the AxPact Project Governance Initiative. Keith still works hands on in the sale and governance of AX delivery projects through his own company ERP Advisers Ltd, including being the lead project manager/project governor on a number of complex AX implementations.

I would like to thank everyone who has supported me in this endeavor, including my family and especially my lovely wife Ann, Chandru Shankar, my brother Andrew Dunkinson, Stephen Holden at Fulcrum, Clare Morrissey, and everyone who has helped me along the way in the last couple of decades, not forgetting my professional lifetime mentor Alan Hindley.

Andrew Birch has over fifteen years experience in the technology industry, starting his career as a network infrastructure engineer before moving to an operations management position in a software development company. Andrew began working with AX (Axapta) in 2003, and has since become one of the foremost proponents of Dynamics AX in Europe, speaking at several Microsoft events, and his projects have won a top industry award. He has been heavily involved in the creation and implementation of Microsoft Dynamics AX add-ons, particularly for the feed industry, that focus on real-time integrations between AX and production control systems. Andrew is now the lead consultant at Binary Consultants, a company he owns and runs with some of the most experienced and creative Dynamics AX and Microsoft .NET professionals in the UK.

I would like to thank all the team at Binary Consultants, especially Simon Buxton and Josh Townson for their technical insight, engaging debate, and furious desire to be proved right, which is what drives Binary forward, and has given me the knowledge (along with the things I was right about) to write this book. I'd also like to thank Clare Morrissey for her dedicated proof reading and relentless reminders about deadlines, without which this book would be neither comprehendible nor finished!

About the Reviewers

Simon Buxton started his IT career as database developer, writing bespoke database systems for printing, and later for financial accounting customers. Working for small companies required him to become capable in all aspects of solution design, build and delivery; which was a good grounding for when he became Technical Director (and sole 'technical' employee) of a new Dynamics AX reseller 'Sense Enterprise Solutions'.

He joined Sense Enterprise Solutions (SES) after a year working for Columbus IT Partner as one of their team leaders, where one of the first UK installations of AX (Axapta 1.5) was completed for a local distributor.

The projects won by SES were typically more technically challenging than usual. This experience found him consultancy projects from Bahrain to the USA.

The solutions often included much wider use of technology than normally encountered and involved developing solutions for third party logistics, multichannel retail, and eventually developing an Animal Feed vertical, integrating Dynamics AX into production control systems, government gateways, ecommerce solutions, and myriad others.

Currently working as a Technical Solution Architect at Binary Consultants, he is passionate about solution design and conforming to the best practices of solution design and delivery. He also believes strongly that this comes from the way the delivery partner is run, its ethos and internal efficiency.

Marco A. Carvalho is from the United States. He has been working with Dynamics AX since 2003, when it was originally called Axapta and has never looked back since. For many years, Marco has worked to start up VARs in Dynamics AX, primarily focusing on its technological capabilities and helping educate businesses about the product. He is currently a Manager of Consulting Services at Junction Solutions, a leading Gold Certified Microsoft Partner. He is also a published author himself, having written the very successful Dynamics AX 2009 Administration book.

I would like to thank my family and friends who have always been supportive and have shown true unconditional love and patience through my entire career. I would also like to provide a shout out to the Junction Book Club!

Angela McClelland is a Software Developer and Technical Consultant for Dynamics AX (AX), currently working as a freelance consultant in the United Kingdom.

Angela began working with AX in 2001, while completing a Computer Science degree at The University of Waikato in New Zealand. After a successful implementation of version 2.5, and later upgrade to 3, the spouse and bags were packed up and moved over to England to seek out bigger project challenges, and for a taste of world travel.

Since this move, Angela has worked on many AX implementations, specializing in business solutions design, X++ programming, Reporting and Business Intelligence. She is a Microsoft Certified Professional for AX: Development, Installation and Configuration, as well as key modules: Finance, Projects, Production, Trade & Logistics, and is also a Microsoft Certified Trainer for AX.

A big thanks to the authors for all the effort in writing this book, and for inviting me to be one of the reviewers. I've learned many things.

David Probst, with a background in Economics and Computer Science, has been working professionally with Microsoft Dynamics AX since 2001, focusing on specific modules including CRM, Service Management, Shop Floor Control, Environmental Sustainability, Inventory management, and Quality management.

Mohammed Rasheed is a Dynamics AX Solutions Architect, and is responsible for design, delivery, and quality of interfaces and customizations on Dynamics AX. Mohammed's core focus at the moment is Dynamics AX for retail, as he leads one of the largest retail implementations in the UK.

Mohammed lives with his wife Sakeena in Chester, UK.

Table of Contents

Preface

This book provides a comprehensive guide to implementing Microsoft Dynamics AX 2012 with Sure Step 2012, and is the perfect accompaniment for project team members of all levels. With discussions on the Diagnostic, Analysis, Design, Development, Deployment, and Operation phases of an implementation project, details of technical concepts that help you effectively manage a project, and real-world examples and hints, managing and delivering successful projects has never been easier!

What this book covers

Chapter 1, Installing and Setting up Sure Step, examines the installation of Sure Step and the setup of projects, and discusses the project offerings that are available within Sure Step.

Chapter 2, The Diagnostic, introduces you to the Diagnostic phase of a Sure Step implementation project, where we identify the overlap with the sales process, understand and choose Decision Accelerators and initiate project management and governance.

Chapter 3, Planning the Infrastructure to Support Dynamics AX, will help you to discover when and how you should start planning your infrastructure, how to choose the best technologies and roles for your project, and how to get the most out of your project team.

Chapter 4, Installing the Dynamics AX Environments, will help you in understanding the key factors that influence how and when you get started in installing your Dynamics AX environments, which can have a major influence on the overall success of your project. Here we offer tips and advice on how to manage this stage effectively.

Chapter 5, Business Requirements Analysis, will introduce you to the key objectives of the Analysis phase, including help in ensuring that the detailed business requirements have been properly scoped and understood and all contractual documentation is in place. This chapter will guide you through these important steps with helpful hints and examples.

Chapter 6, AX Setup, will help you to find out the basic setup required to make AX useable, and gain insights into the system configuration. This chapter will help you make the right decisions when it comes to setting up AX correctly.

Chapter 7, Integration, will discuss the importance of creating an integration plan for third party software systems, and help you plan and test effectively.

Chapter 8, Harnessing the Power of Standard AX Features, will help you to discover the wealth of highly configurable standard features available to you in AX that allow you to tailor the applications without modification or customization, and find out how to get the best out of AX without development.

Chapter 9, Designing and Developing the Solution, will help you get creative with the design of the AX solution, understand the impact of making changes to AX and know when to develop and when not to. This chapter will guide you through the solution design and assist you with the planning of the development.

Chapter 10, Reports, Document Layouts, and Business Intelligence, will help you learn the differences between Reports, Document Layouts, and Business Intelligence, and discover how to analyze and plan for their implementation.

Chapter 11, Deployment Phase, will increase your confidence in your deployment, after having analyzed, designed, and developed your AX solution. This chapter provides information on End User Training, User Acceptance Testing, Data Migration, and the Cutover to the new system.

Chapter 12, Project Governance and Quality Assurance, will help you with the extensive Project Governance and Quality Assurance that is becoming more and more necessary for larger projects. This chapter will also help you discover more about conducting project lifecycle reviews, auditing, and creating quality review plans.

Chapter 13, Operation Phase, will guide you, following months of planning and design, through the final stages of the project and the most exciting stage—handing the completed system over to a happy customer and transitioning the solution to support. This chapter will also help you learn about the important planning that goes into this stage, and how to have a successful go-live!

What you need for this book

In order to appreciate this book fully, we recommend you have a version of the Sure Step 2012 client, which can be downloaded from PartnerSource or CustomerSource. It is advantageous that you have a copy of AX 2012, or at least a working knowledge of Dynamics AX.

Who this book is for

Implementing Microsoft Dynamics AX 2012 with Sure Step 2012 will help you better understand the principles of Sure Step methodology, and enable you to utilize these in a practical and pragmatic way when implementing Microsoft Dynamics AX 2012. Not only will you increase your knowledge and insights into each of the Sure Step Implementation phases and the AX application itself, you will gain the confidence to deal with the unexpected and problematic. With examples of real-life projects and helpful hints and tips, this book will help you become a skilled project manager able to deliver managed expectations on time, on budget! This book is detailed enough for novices or those new to Microsoft Dynamics implementation projects, and also covers topics that benefit more experienced project team members.

Conventions

In this book, you will find a number of styles of text that distinguish between different kinds of information. Here are some examples of these styles, and an explanation of their meaning.

Code words in text are shown as follows: "The most common file type, for example `.doc`, `.docx`, `.xls`, `.xlsx`, `.pdf`, and so on, are preconfigured, but if you plan to upload files generated by specialist applications, you may need to add their file extensions to the list."

New terms and **important words** are shown in bold. Words that you see on the screen, in menus or dialog boxes for example, appear in the text like this: "To create a project, run the Sure Step client and select the **Projects** tab from the opening screen.".

> Warnings or important notes appear in a box like this.

> Tips and tricks appear like this.

Reader feedback

Feedback from our readers is always welcome. Let us know what you think about this book—what you liked or may have disliked. Reader feedback is important for us to develop titles that you really get the most out of.

To send us general feedback, simply send an e-mail to `feedback@packtpub.com`, and mention the book title via the subject of your message.

If there is a book that you need and would like to see us publish, please send us a note in the **SUGGEST A TITLE** form on `www.packtpub.com` or e-mail `suggest@packtpub.com`.

If there is a topic that you have expertise in and you are interested in either writing or contributing to a book, see our author guide on `www.packtpub.com/authors`.

Customer support

Now that you are the proud owner of a Packt book, we have a number of things to help you to get the most from your purchase.

Errata

Although we have taken every care to ensure the accuracy of our content, mistakes do happen. If you find a mistake in one of our books—maybe a mistake in the text or the code—we would be grateful if you would report this to us. By doing so, you can save other readers from frustration and help us improve subsequent versions of this book. If you find any errata, please report them by visiting `http://www.packtpub.com/support`, selecting your book, clicking on the **errata submission form** link, and entering the details of your errata. Once your errata are verified, your submission will be accepted and the errata will be uploaded on our website, or added to any list of existing errata, under the Errata section of that title. Any existing errata can be viewed by selecting your title from `http://www.packtpub.com/support`.

Piracy

Piracy of copyright material on the Internet is an ongoing problem across all media. At Packt, we take the protection of our copyright and licenses very seriously. If you come across any illegal copies of our works, in any form, on the Internet, please provide us with the location address or website name immediately so that we can pursue a remedy.

Please contact us at `copyright@packtpub.com` with a link to the suspected pirated material.

We appreciate your help in protecting our authors, and our ability to bring you valuable content.

Questions

You can contact us at `questions@packtpub.com` if you are having a problem with any aspect of the book, and we will do our best to address it.

1
Installing and Setting up Sure Step

In this chapter, we will examine the installation of Sure Step and setting it up for a specific project including some of the key choices we need to make, and activities that should be undertaken at this time. After reading this chapter, we should be able to: download and install the Sure Step client, create an appropriate Sure Step project, and initiate key activities for our Dynamics AX project.

Sure Step is the methodology created by Microsoft for implementing Dynamics projects. Although Sure Step includes content for Dynamics: NAV, AX, GP, SL, and CRM, our book is only focusing on AX. In some cases, one Dynamics project will be split into multiple Sure Step projects. This may be the case for projects covering one or more phases or for global rollouts, with sub-projects covering multiple territories or lines of business.

Sure Step has evolved through several versions, and gains content and maturity through each one. There would be no need to use an earlier version, so we have only considered the current version in this book (Sure Step 2010).

Sure Step is designed to be used by both customers and partners, and although it is currently most often used by partners, it is becoming more and more common for customers to follow Sure Step methodology when implementing ERP systems. In this book, we use "project" to describe an implementation of Microsoft Dynamics AX. In most cases, one Microsoft Dynamics AX project will be the subject of one Microsoft Sure Step project.

For more comprehensive information on Sure Step, you should refer the Microsoft training materials, or the *Packt Publishing* title *Microsoft Dynamics Sure Step 2010 ISBN 978-1-849681-10-0* by *Chandru Shankar* and *Vincent Bellefroid*.

This chapter will introduce the Sure Step methodology, explain how to install the Sure Step client and create new projects, discuss the various engagement and project types that are available within Sure Step, and explore the steps that need to be taken during the project initiation phase.

Installing Sure Step

Sure Step is available to Microsoft Dynamics customers and partners via download from the Microsoft CustomerSource or PartnerSource portals respectively. The download and installation of Sure Step is simple and similar to installing other Microsoft desktop applications. For this reason, step-by-step instructions will not be detailed here, however, this information can be found in the instructions that accompany the download.

Creating the Dynamics AX project

Once the Sure Step client is installed, it is time to create a project for a Microsoft Dynamics AX implementation. To create a project, run the Sure Step client and select the **Projects** tab from the opening screen.

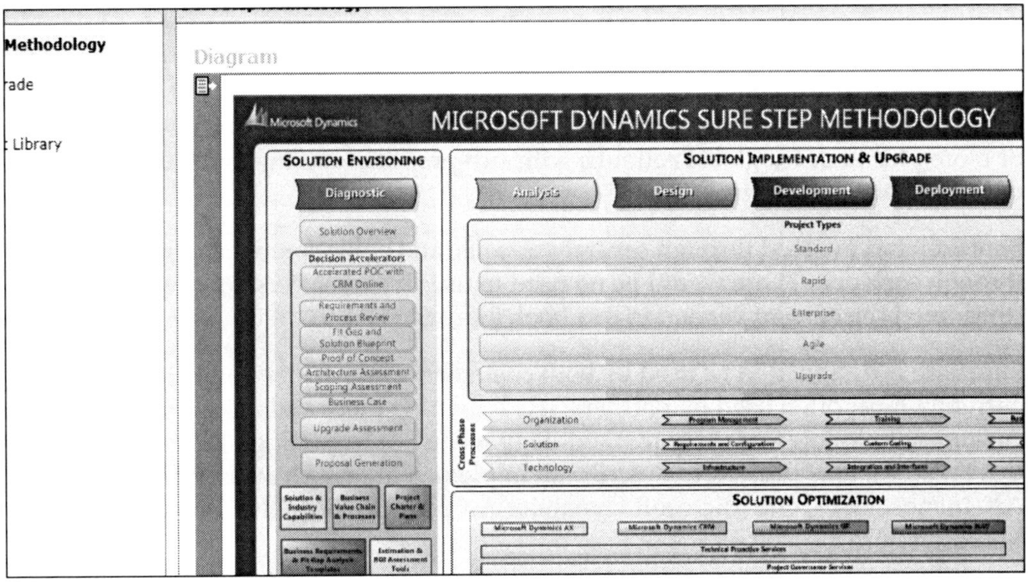

Once the **Project** tab is selected there is a list of existing projects. Upon choosing the option **Create New Project**, a wizard guides us through the creation process.

The first stage of the wizard asks us to enter the project data as shown in the following screenshot:

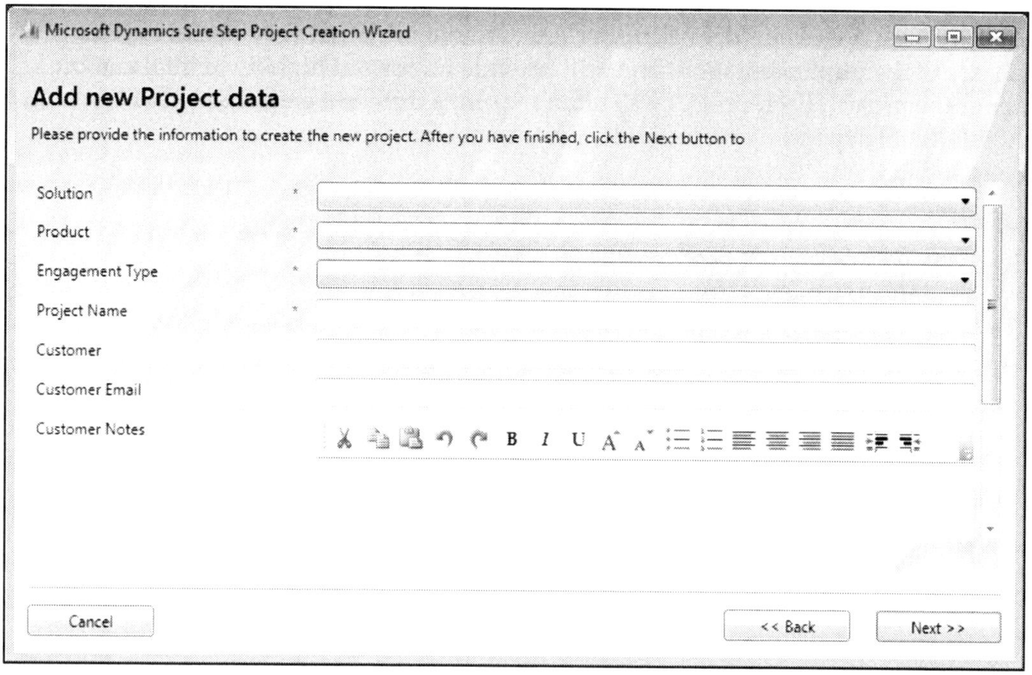

The fields marked with a red asterisk (*) are mandatory.

The solution and product are obvious and the project name is a matter of personal preference, but the engagement is worthy of an explanation and is detailed in the following sections.

Engagement types (offerings)

Engagement types refer to the choice of **Diagnostic**, **Implementation**, or **Optimization** offerings.

Diagnostic phase offering

Selecting a Diagnostic phase offering creates a Sure Step project, with content and guidance exclusively covering solution envisioning (Diagnostic activities). This allows the partner and customer to gain a high-level understanding of the fit of the solution to the customers' needs, which in turn allows the partner to be able to define the scope, cost, and risk of the implementation more effectively. This type of offering is therefore, intended to be used by a partner to increase their customers' confidence in, and commitment to, an implementation of a Dynamics product.

If a Diagnostic offering is chosen, there is the option of including one or more of the **Decision Accelerators** pictured in the following screenshot. **Decision Accelerators** such as **Requirements and Process Review, Fit Gap and Solution Blueprint, Architecture Assessment**, or **Scoping Assessment** are often very useful in later phases of the implementation, and will provide important high-level information about the project. Each project will often require a different combination of Decision Accelerators depending on individual circumstances, and more details on these can be found in the next chapter.

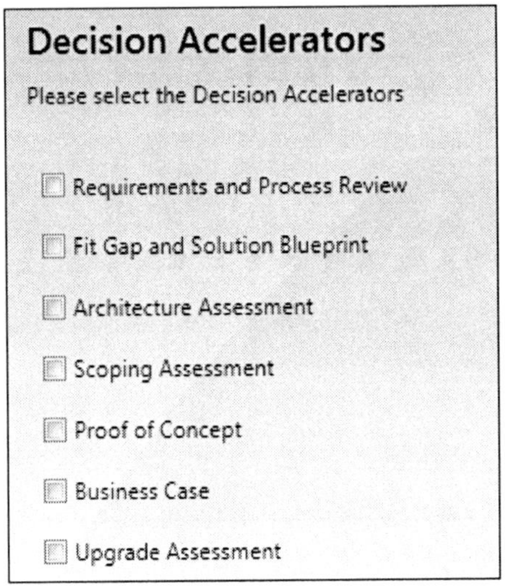

Implementation offering

Selecting an Implementation offering creates a project, with content and guidance covering the full project implementation including the envisioning (Diagnostics) phase. This includes the key phases, namely **Analysis**, **Design**, **Development**, and **Deployment**. The Sure Step implementation project is intended to be used to help a customer (who would normally be working with a partner) to successfully implement a Dynamics project, and is the case we are considering in this book.

Optimization offering

Selecting this option creates a Sure Step project, with content and guidance covering the upgrade or improvement of an existing system. As the fundamentals of the upgrade template are covered in the implementation template, we will not be specifically covering the optimization in this book.

Project types

Depending on which Engagement Type we have chosen, Sure Step will now require entry of a project type on the next step of the wizard. Typically, we will choose an Implementation offering, which is the template that will be covered in the scope of this book. The five project types (Rapid, Standard, Enterprise, Agile, and Optimization) are described in the following sections. This is a very important choice, because the content and guidance for the project types differ markedly.

The typical project types are Rapid, Standard, and Enterprise, all of which are referred to as waterfall project types, as they follow discrete sequential phases as shown in the following screenshot:

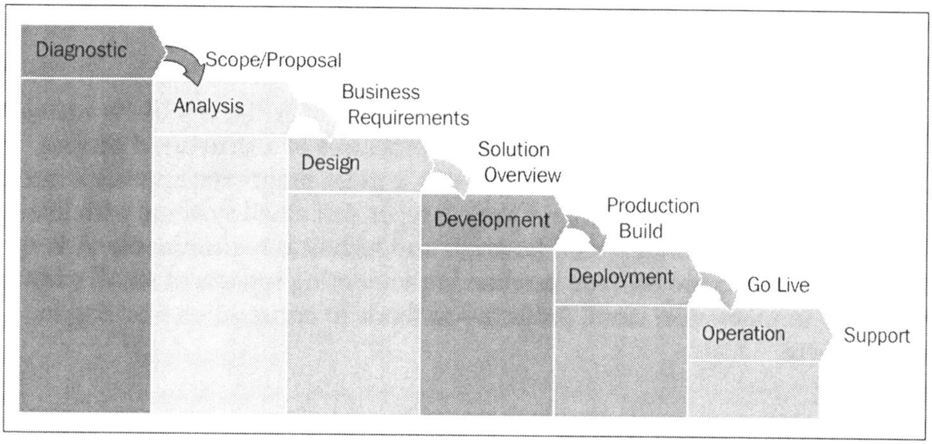

Choosing a project type requires both subjective and objective evaluation of the risk and complexity of a project. Subjective analysis should include an assessment of the capability of the project teams, the buy-in of senior management, budget and timescale constraints, and so on. When looking back at challenged projects, the choice of too lightweight a project type is often cited as the reason for failure. When choosing the project type, projects have generally not yet encountered difficulties, and often budget and timescale constraints can be given too much weight in making the choice of project type. As the decision includes subjective and objective evaluation, it is ultimately a subjective choice which the project manager or governance team needs to be prepared to be accountable for.

Some objective analysis points are identified in the following table:

Project type	Business Process Analysis	Lines Of Business	Sites	Users	Fit to the Gap Fit	ISV solutions	Complexity	Countries
Rapid	No	1	1	1-35	>90 percent	0	Low	1
Standard	Some	1-2	1-3	25-250	>75 percent	1	Medium	1-5
Enterprise	Extensive	>1	3+	250+	<75 percent	>1	High	5+
Agile	No	1+	1+	1+	<75 percent	1+	Medium	1+

Rapid project type

A Rapid project type will be created using the minimum artifacts (objects such as documents, spreadsheets, and diagrams) and processes of a structured project. As the project has less complexity and less risk, a more pragmatic approach can be taken to manage the project. Rapid project types suit small systems with little customization and well understood business and technical requirements. A very good use of the Rapid project type is when implementing repeats or small variations of previously implemented small projects—as tends to occur when working in vertical markets.

Standard project type

A Standard project type will be created with more artifacts, particularly around business process analysis and project governance. These suit more typical AX projects. Standard projects suit typical AX implementations with one or two sites, perhaps an **Independent Software Vendor** (**ISV**) solution and some customization.

Enterprise project type

An Enterprise project type will have the maximum number of artifacts and content based around quality assurance, governance, communications management, and all the elements required for managing large teams delivering complicated projects.

Enterprise project suit more complex projects. Complexity is a bit subjective as it is influenced by all of the factors in the following list, but most of them on their own don't necessarily make a project an Enterprise project.

- International
- Multi-site

- Complex modifications
- Multiple ISV solutions
- Organizational Change Management
- Business Process Reengineering

It is simple in Sure Step to create fictitious projects of all these types to review the content differences, which can be done using the Sure Step client.

Agile project type

The Agile project type is based on a wholly different approach to projects than the previous types. The previous types are all waterfall methodologies, where one stage is completed before progressing to the next stage through a familiar model of diagnosis, analysis, design, development, and deployment.

A typical Agile project type follows an iterative approach shown in the following screenshot:

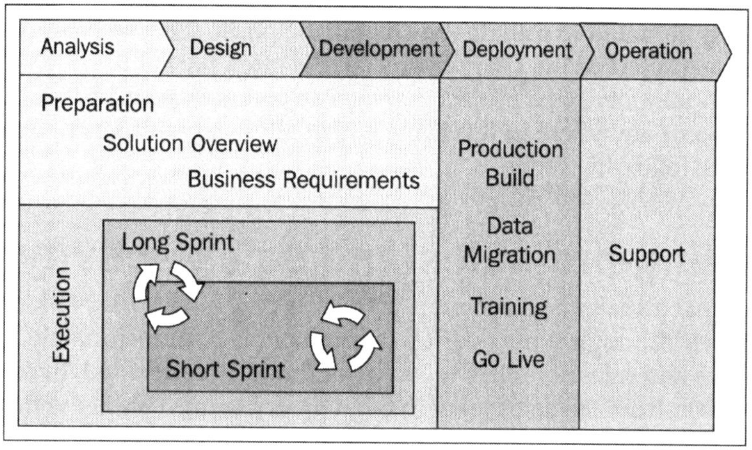

An Agile project does not follow the waterfall type of approach and lacks some of the structure and stages of these types of projects. In an Agile project, an initial Diagnostic activity will occur, followed by an Agile Preparation phase. This will be followed by iterative cycles of **Analysis**, **Design**, and **Development**, known as **sprint cycles**. Each sprint cycle will focus on a pre-agreed list of activities, and anything outstanding at the end of that sprint cycle will be assigned to a later sprint cycle. There will be major sprint cycles (typically monthly) and minor sprint cycles (typically daily). At the start of each sprint cycle, there will be a sprint cycle review meeting to agree a list of activities to include and to provide an update on progress.

Agile projects tend to be used where requirements are not sufficiently detailed but the project needs to get started, or where requirements are frequently changing. They are therefore iterative and their duration is hard to predict. This makes them difficult to manage and they should be avoided by inexperienced project managers. Even in an Agile project, it is important to ensure that activities from a Standard project type (testing, training, data migration, and so on) are completed and managed properly.

Upgrade project type

It is slightly odd that having not chosen an Optimization Engagement Type, you are nevertheless offered an Upgrade project type even for an Implementation offering. We will ignore this for the purposes of this book, which is about implementing AX, not upgrading it.

Project initiation

Project initiation is expected to occur between the Diagnostic and Analysis phases. On a larger project, each phase requires some initiation activity of its own and it is particularly common to initiate the Diagnostic phase separately from the Implementation project as the Diagnostic phase is often part of the decision making process. The appointment of a project manager to commence end-to-end planning activities can occur anywhere in this cycle which obviously influences initiation as discussed in the following sections.

Concluding pre-sales and sales activity

It is desirable that all sales and pre-sales activity is concluded prior to kicking off the main project, although some overlap is common. It is, unfortunately, not rare for the pre-sales and sales activities to have not formally concluded, or to have been handed over from the sales team to the delivery team. This is the first thing a project manager should be chasing and why we have emphasized it here. See the relevant Sure Step details, but at this stage a Project Charter, Statement of Work, Implementation Contract, Proposal, and Requirements review are among the key minimum requirements to plan a project.

Document repository

As both the partner and client project teams need to share documents and files, we should provide a repository. Not all content should be visible to all users of the repository, so appropriate security controls or multiple repositories need to be considered.

Setting up the repository early in the project provides useful structure and saves hunting for current versions of documents later in the project. Microsoft SharePoint and/or SharePoint Workspace should suffice, although there are numerous options.

Although there are many Sure Step documents, in this book we want to consider some of the most important and most overlooked, that in our project experience, can help make the difference between managed expectations or a degree of failure. Accordingly, below we have identified some of the first items that belong in the document repository.

Communication plan

The communication plan should be one of the first documents in the repository and Sure Step provides a good template document for this.

The plan identifies all key project documents and communication types (for example, meetings). From within the plan, we can see the current version of all documents and communications, who last edited them and who is responsible for them. In addition, adding a URL to anything that has an associated file is a good practice for easy reference. Early in the project, this provides an index to key project files and documentation and should be maintained throughout the project.

Project hierarchy, communications, and meetings

Project hierarchy refers to the tiers of management governing a project. It is vital to establish the governance at the outset of the project and clearly communicate it to the whole project team—one of the functions of the communication plan.

Different projects will require different governance structures depending on risk, size of the project, project type, project duration, and so on. This should be established as soon as the project kicks off and evolved during the project, if necessary. Each of the governance groups should attend a kick-off meeting of the project, and in larger projects, kick-off meetings of every phase. These meetings can be separate or combined as is appropriate.

It is most common to have three levels of governance, whose team members overlap a little as shown in the following screenshot:

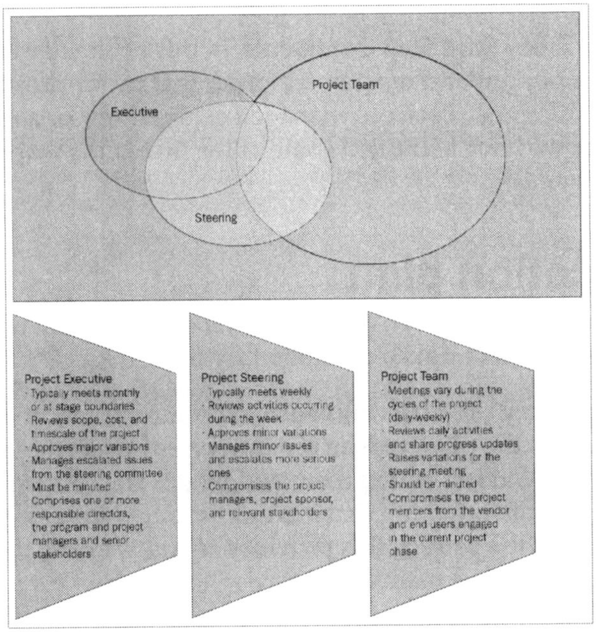

Statement of Work and Project Charter

Several documents are required at the outset of the project. The Statement of Work (normally provided by the partner) lists the scope of the key deliverables of the project. The Project Charter lists the rules of engagement of a project. These are supplemented by the System Proposal and Project Contract, but most of the time, the high-level scope can be checked from these two documents. Sure Step provides good templates for these.

Functional Requirements Document

The **Functional Requirements Document** (**FRD**) is a more obvious document and is perhaps the most important project document which details scope at a functional level. Most projects do contain an FRD, but in retrospective evaluation, they often lack some of the detail required. The FRD should contain all of the customer's requirements listed from a process or functional perspective. Each requirement should be listed in sufficient detail to satisfy the project team members from the customer and partner that the requirement is well enough understood to agree scope against. Each requirement should be identifiable via a reference which can be cross-referenced from the Gap Fit, Software Design Specifications, and so on.

Non-functional requirements

Non-functional requirements are also captured such as technical environment, high availability, migration, and so on. This is covered in the later chapters.

Other documents

The Gap Fit, which records the level of fit of requirements to the standard application, is a simple but important document; this is rarely lacking in a project, so we have not focussed on it here. There are many other documents we could mention, but if we look at the **Documents** tab of the Sure Step projects created earlier in this chapter, we can see and learn more about them there.

Work Breakdown Structure

The **Work Breakdown Structure** (**WBS**) is an entity used to link activities for the purposes of measurement and management. Sure Step includes a template WBS, but we may make our own if we feel it would be more suitable to the project. The benefits of having a clear and defined WBS from the beginning of the project are often realized in later stages, when reporting on the progress and budget to key stakeholders becomes more important. Three examples of structures are provided in the following tables. WBS 3 is the only one extracted from Sure Step; the others are examples of alternatives.

WBS 1 Worker Based Single Level:

WBS Level	Resource	Name
1	Consultant 1	Andrew Birch
2	Consultant 2	Keith Dunkinson
3	Consultant 3	Andrew Dunkinson

WBS 2 Worker Based Two Levels:

WBS Level	Resource	Name	Activity
1.1	Consultant 1	Andrew Birch	Analysis
1.2	Consultant 1	Andrew Birch	Design
2.1	Consultant 1	Andrew Birch	Development
2.2	Consultant 2	Keith Dunkinson	Analysis
2.3	Consultant 2	Keith Dunkinson	Design
2.4	Consultant 2	Keith Dunkinson	Development

Sure Step provides good templates for WBS including the following one:

WBS 3 Extract of Sure Step Enterprise 4 level WBS:

WBS Level	Activity
1	Sure Step Enterprise methodology
1.1	Analysis phase
1.1.0	Program management
1.1.1	Project planning
1.1.1.1	Conduct Executive kick-off
• E1.1.1.1	• Executive kick-off meeting
1.1.1.2	Develop Organizational Change Management Strategy
• E1.1.1.2	• Organizational Change Management Strategy
• 1.1.1.3	• Develop leadership action plan
• E1.1.1.3	• Leadership action plan
• 1.1.1.4	• Finalize Project Charter
• E1.1.1.4	• Project Charter
• 1.1.1.5	• Finalize WBS and project plan
• E1.1.1.5	• Project plan
• 1.1.1.6	• Review and Approve Project Charter and project plan
• 1.1.2	• Risks and issues management
• 1.1.2.1	• Conduct Organization risk and readiness assessment
• E1.1.2.1	• Organization risk and readiness assessment analysis
• E1.1.2.2	• Risk and readiness assessment report

Linking the WBS to planning activities, progress, budgets, and the timesheets enables close cost control and duration management of the project.

WBS levels

We may measure and manage at any level of the WBS, but what we must consider with using detailed levels is that activities and budgets then need to be planned and recorded at the same level of granularity. We can of course manage different things using different levels of WBS, but again, consideration is required to ensure they can be reconciled at an appropriate level of detail.

Labor and materials tracking

Reconciling progress and budgets requires collecting information at the appropriate level of detail. Therefore, the budgeting formats and timesheets need to be agreed before the project begins. All too often, this is not realized until after the project has commenced and reconciliation has already become futile.

Time logs

In particular, timesheets from the consulting team (or indeed any budgeted resource) need to be broken down into the level of reporting required. This can be difficult for resources who undertake a wide range of activities in a day, and this should also be considered when planning the granularity of measurement and management required.

Initiating Cross Phase activities

While we have covered some of the more important and arguably less common activities, there are of course many more we could have considered. The project type, our project's needs, and our own experience will influence choices, and adoption of methodology for the project. Sure Step includes good content for Cross Phase activities, project type selection, Organizational Change Management, and so on. Once we have made our decisions, we should look again at what Sure Step has suggested before setting them in stone. If we are not sure, we can seek peer review. There are numerous forums for Sure Step and experts are available to help if necessary. The Microsoft forums, LinkedIn Dynamics World, and Mibuso are all useful reference points.

Summary

Sure Step is readily available to Microsoft Dynamics partners and customers and can easily be installed and set up. Utilising Sure Step appropriately requires experience of implementing Dynamics projects in a structured fashion.

In a Dynamics AX context, Sure Step includes content and guidance covering:

- **Phases**: This section explains how a project type goes through iterative cycles, such as Diagnostic, Analysis, Design, Deployment, and Operation.
- **Project types**: This section describes different project types, namely Rapid, Standard, Enterprise, and Agile.

  - **Cross Phase activities**: This section provides information on how Cross Phase activities are configured using Sure Step, which are listed as follows:
    - **Organization**: Program Management, Training, Business Process Analysis.
    - **Solution**: Requirements and Configuration, Custom Coding, Quality and Testing.
    - **Technology**: Infrastructure, Integrations and Interfaces, Data Migration.
  - **Project Management Library**: This section provides information on and best practices for standard activities that are carried out by project management throughout a project.
  - **Organizational Change Management Library**: This section provides a blueprint of the approach to Change Management for the project.
  - **Role identification**: This section provides an overview of the customer and consultant roles that are involved in a Dynamics implementation.
  - **Solution optimization**: The different types of solutions available are described in this section, which is listed as follows:
    - **Solution types**: General; Manufacturing, Public Sector, Retail Industries, Service Industries, and Customer Care.

Project initiation activities should be considered very early in a project, as they are much harder to implement properly once a project has started without them.

Every project is unique and while trying to conform to standards, we need to be flexible and dynamic in our approach to achieve the best results within a reasonable timescale and cost.

In this chapter, we have introduced you to the Sure Step client and discussed the various Engagement and project types available. We have also outlined the activities needed to move an engagement from the pre-sales phase on to the implementation phase. In the next chapter, we will cover the Diagnostic phase, including Decision Accelerators, cross-phase activities and third party products.

2 The Diagnostic

This chapter will focus on finding a path through the Sure Step Diagnostic offering, including a worked example. In a Diagnostic, Sure Step offers many components to consider, which need combining into a single offering. This can overlap with the selling phase, which requires some special consideration. Points to be covered in this chapter include:

- Overlapping the Diagnostic phase with sales process
- Understanding and choosing Decision Accelerators
- When/why to prototype
- Initiating project management and governance
- Working as a team to deliver a Diagnostic phase
- Diagnostic review and sign off
- Vertical markets and third party products

Overlapping with the sales phase

A customer will normally initiate an activity to implement an ERP system internally. Sometimes this is the first such system for a customer, but more normally it will be the replacement of one or more existing systems.

During the initial consideration, a customer will typically identify many possible systems and narrow them down to a long list. Often with few formal criteria, a shortlist of those systems that are perceived to be able to meet the customer's needs, will be created. As the customer begins to consider how to select one system from another in more detail, they will usually engage a client side project manager and produce formal criteria for selection. The formal criteria may include: a **Pre-Qualification Questionnaire** (**PQQ**), and/or an **Invitation to Tender** document (**ITT**), or similar. Often, even after several systems have been evaluated, there will still be more than one contender to choose from.

Microsoft Solution Selling Process (**MSSP**) and Microsoft Dynamics Sure Step dovetail areas of content for helping customers narrow down their product selection. The intention is to provide enough confidence to the customer during the sales process that they can comfortably commit to implementing a Microsoft Dynamics solution, in our case Dynamics AX.

The salesperson's intention is to move the customer from the customer buying cycle into the partner selling cycle. Diagnostic is the tool to achieve this. The Microsoft Sure Step Diagnostic phase contains a number of optional components quite literally called Decision Accelerators. The Decision Accelerators are designed to examine a customer's requirements, and/or obstacles to purchase, and match them to the proposed solution.

Sometimes a Diagnostic is a paid engagement and sometimes it is a free of charge or partially chargeable presales activity. When the Diagnostic is a paid engagement, the customer may have already chosen the Dynamics solution, and is merely looking to validate their decision prior to a complete contractual commitment. Where a Diagnostic is unpaid, often the customer is still looking to make a decision and leans towards the Diagnostic in order to achieve what the buying cycle has not. When a customer has not made a decision, they may want their Diagnostic to be solution agnostic, but often a customer is happy to have a Diagnostic biased towards their preferred solution. Some Decision Accelerators need to be product specific.

It should be clear from the above that the Diagnostic may commence during the sales cycle and this should be borne in mind. In the more preferable case that the sales cycle is effectively over and we are transitioning through Diagnostic into a project, it is more acceptable to bring in more project structure and governance. Typically, the project is not sold and does not formally start (under agreed contracts) until the Analysis phase. This matters because it is important to focus the Diagnostic around the customer and partners needs, and the stage of the selling cycle can make a big difference to the focus.

In any case, it is common for the project team not to be engaged until the Diagnostic or even the Analysis phase. In these cases, it is very important to ensure that the handover from the sales team to the project team, possibly via the diagnostic team, is very well documented. The Sure Step document types in each phase allow this, but the project manager has to be on the ball to ensure that the customers' expectations as well as the partner's promises are well understood and clearly documented. The Diagnostic contains key tools to achieve this.

At the end of the Diagnostics phase, the customer will normally choose to engage with the Diagnostic vendor to implement Microsoft Dynamics AX. If the Diagnostic does not provide evidence that Microsoft Dynamics AX is the right solution, a step back to considering other systems may also be necessary.

A process for selection from among multiple Microsoft Dynamics AX partners is something for the customer to consider, but we would advocate including the following in the selection process:

- Experience of the partner in customers' industry
- Financial stability of partner
- Stability and expertise of the partner's team
- Availability of preferred staff for your project
- Commercial terms
- Not just prices, but the basis for the prices; consider the following:
    - Daily rate
    - Overtime rates
    - Hours per working day
    - Contract details, such as Ownership of Intellectual Property, Payment Terms, and Cancellation Terms
    - Fixed Price or Time and Materials or Fixed Price per Scope
- Ability to deliver on time
- Customer references (pick your own, not necessarily those suggested)
- Certification by Microsoft (Gold Certified, CfMD, Inner Circle Presidents Club, AMR Industry certification)

One service the authors often provide to customers is assistance in choosing a partner.

Decision accelerators

Sure Step includes a range of **Decision Accelerators**, which are combined to create a Diagnostic phase offering for a client. The following list shows the eight available accelerators from the Sure Step client:

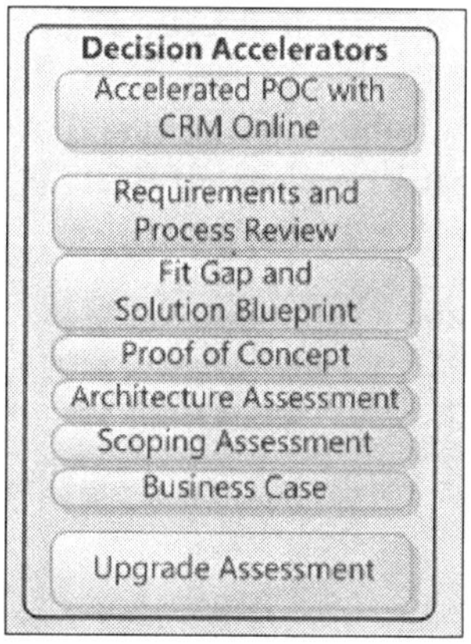

The quantity and mix of Decision Accelerators is the first thing that needs to be identified for the Diagnostic. The choice should be focused upon what is necessary to prove that we are offering the right solution, and allow that to be unequivocally documented to the customer and partner's satisfaction. The degree of fit of the standard product, the size and complexity of the project, the budget, and the timescale available are all the factors which will contribute in making this decision. Reading the descriptions of the Decision Accelerators in the following sections should help us to choose Decision Accelerators to meet our needs.

Accelerated Proof of Concept (POC) with CRM online

The **Accelerated Proof of Concept** (**POC**) with CRM online is only relevant to Dynamics CRM and out of the scope of this book. It is of course possible to implement Dynamics CRM alongside Dynamics AX but, we consider them to be separately linked projects.

Requirements and Process Review

The Requirements and Process Review is a part of most Diagnostics. Occasionally, the customer's tender process will have already sufficiently identified the requirements and processes and obviate the need for repeating this in the Diagnostic. Even more rarely, the customers' requirements may be very unclear leading to an iterative requirements clarification approach suiting an agile project type.

Normally, a Requirements and Process Review will be required and its aim will be to identify and review the high-level requirements and processes that are expected to be included in the new ERP system. It is worth noting that Sure Step does not demand that the requirements and processes are fully documented, that is the purpose of the Analysis phase. The focus is on identifying requirements and processes in sufficient detail so that their degree of fit and inclusion in project scope can be determined from the Diagnostic phase. Note the potential overlap with Business Process Reengineering, which is discussed in *Chapter 7, Integration*. In the Diagnostic phase, we should focus on **Current State** (**CS**) processes, **Future State** (**FS**) processes will be considered in a later phase.

The requirements should at least consider integration and non-functional requirements, but it should also be agreed whether they go as far as identifying the following:

- Role centers
- Security
- Workflows
- Data migration
- Reporting and document layouts
- Training needs
- Testing requirements and responsibilities
- Project management

We refer to these items as areas of variable scope, and they can have a huge impact on budget and timescales. It is a frequent misunderstanding of expectations that the partner expects the customer to perform these, while the customer expects the partner to perform them. They may well be the subject of the other Decision Accelerators, particularly the Scoping Assessment. What matters most is that it is made clear that these have not had special consideration at this time as their inclusion later will most certainly affect project time and cost planning.

Fit Gap and Solutions Blueprint

The purpose of the Fit Gap and Solutions Blueprint is to compare the requirements identified with the Microsoft Dynamics solution and identify what, if any, customization and configuration is necessary to fulfil those gaps.

The Fit Gap is a spreadsheet on which all the customers' requirements are identified, and the degree of system customization and configuration necessary to meet these requirements is estimated. This is subtotalled to provide metrics for estimating and planning the project against.

The Solution Blueprint is a report which covers the understanding of requirements and fit including key conceptual design considerations and any assumptions made.

Proof of Concept

A **Proof of Concept** (POC) accelerator is an examination of the system's fit to specific customer requirements via an extended demonstration of the software. The POC would be more thorough than a simple presales demonstration. The biggest difference in a presales demonstration is a focus on clearly identifying what is and of course what is not included in the POC. The POC is not a common element of a Diagnostic, but is very useful if the customer needs to see the product working to validate or help make their decision.

A POC often involves a significant amount of effort to install, set up, and demonstrate key business processes. Planning the delivery of the POC should be performed as early as possible as it may take several weeks or more to enact.

Sometimes the need for the POC will have been identified during or following an initial Diagnostic, where the customer has still not made a decision. In this case, it is necessary to update the Fit Gap and any other Diagnostic documents with the results of the POC, if any further requirements or gaps are identified.

Architecture Assessment

Although some consideration to architecture can be included as part of the Solution Blueprint or Scoping Assessment, sometimes it will benefit from being a decision accelerator of its own. On simple projects, the minimum hardware and software specifications make a reasonable basis for suggesting any new architecture requirements the customer may have.

The Architecture Assessment is more focused on planning for the volume of transaction processing the system will perform and assuring predictable performance under high usage conditions. Sure Step includes templates for gathering transaction processing requirements, and these should be considered along with the needs for high availability and disaster recovery.

Assumptions made should be clearly documented, especially where third parties (for example, infrastructure providers) need to respond to the Architecture Assessment.

Scoping Assessment

A Scoping Assessment is a very common element of a Diagnostic—it would be of little use without one. Nevertheless, the details of scope are often left to presentations or proposals, whereas they ought to be provided in a specific Statement of Work which is an essential part of project management and governance. Even where Statements of Work exist, in challenged projects, they are often cited as one of the key problems as they need to be sufficiently detailed and unequivocal. Be sure to include not only what is required, but who is going to provide it.

The Sure Step template contains the following chapter headings:

Chapter	Chapter Heading
1	Executive Summary
2	Project Definition and Objectives
3	Key Deliverables
4	Success Criteria
5	Project Approach
6	Project Scope
7	Scope Change Process
8	Risks
9	Constraints
10	Assumptions

It is worth at this point reviewing the sample document in the Sure Step client if you installed this during *Chapter 1, Installing and Setting up Sure Step*.

The key deliverables in this section involve identifying the contractual control documents and processes of the project, not the requirements, which are of course identified in the Fit Gap.

The success criteria are considered as an important element of Sure Step and contribute greatly to managing scope, customers' expectations, and of course the success of the project.

The scope change process is introduced, as scope is now formally identified, and any change from scope needs documenting properly to save confusion later. Now is definitely the latest point to bring in the formal scope management—the same applies to risk management.

A Scoping Assessment will normally accompany an estimate of cost and time; so a Costing Assessment and Work Breakdown Structure should be introduced at this point and maintained throughout the project. Please also refer to the areas of variable scope identified earlier in this chapter, where we have identified the areas that from our experience are often overlooked. Customization is not listed there, as this is normally identified via some sort of Fit Gap, albeit not always accurately!

Business Case

The Business Case is an examination of the proposed cost of the project with the expected benefits. This is useful in determining **Return on Investment** (**ROI**) metrics and as a compass for comparing scope change requests against. Not all projects or organizations require an ROI assessment, but it needs to be structured where it is required and can be expected to have to stand some scrutiny.

Microsoft has provided access to and guidelines for a Nucleus Return on Investment tool which is well documented within Sure Step. Some organizations will require more thorough consideration than others including, perhaps requiring **Net Present Value** (**NPV**) and **Discounted Cash Flow** (**DCF**) analysis. When offering a business case to the customer, it is wise to do your homework first as it is easy to become embroiled in accounting analysis and value judgements regarding ROI, which is not normally an ERP practitioner's core strength.

Upgrade Assessment

The Upgrade Assessment accelerator purely applies to consideration of upgrades and is not relevant to the scope of this book.

Case study

In the case of the project where we recently implemented Dynamics AX 2012, it was a preferred solution from the outset. The business had recently been acquired and was in the process of changing its management, its systems, and its business processes in the course of adopting an enforced change of direction. The project was a single site rollout of a modified Professional Services Automation project. Every week the new system was delayed, it would incur a significant cost to the business. A Sure Step Agile solution was agreed upon to expedite time and cope with the organizational change that was happening. Although AX was a preferred solution, a Diagnostic was still undertaken to give a basis for scope and costing. Therefore, a Requirements and Process Overview, Architecture Assessment, Scoping Assessment, and Fit Gap were included.

Prototype

Besides a formal proof of concept decision accelerator, we have found it beneficial to create a prototype from the outset of the sales phase. This is useful not only in providing consistent sales demonstrations, but also in interactively discussing issues and concepts with the customer. The loose prototype of the Diagnostic and Analysis phases is normally replaced by the prerelease builds of the solution to be implemented later in the project.

Initiating project management and governance

As discussed previously, the Diagnostic phase more often than not means the project is going to be awarded to the preferred partner. In the old Navision On Target methodology, this would be considered an 80 percent likelihood. It is therefore, a great time to be getting ahead with project initiation activities because when the project kicks off, the pressures and commitments come thick and fast.

Sure Step clearly identifies the need for Cross Phase activities (see the *Summary* section in *Chapter 1, Installing and Setting up Sure Step*) and handily provides much of the material required.

During the Diagnostic, our recommendation is that it is best to focus on setting up the organization, project management, and organizational change management libraries if time permits. In most partner organizations, there should be reasonable templates for most of this, probably based on Sure Step originals.

The Diagnostic itself will have kick-off activities (more of that later in this chapter). Throughout the Diagnostic, regular review points should be scheduled like miniature project status meetings. Treating the Diagnostic like a mini project gives the partner an opportunity to demonstrate their professionalism and the value of their project management services offering.

The content and processes relating to project initiation are easily referenced in the Sure Step client reviewing the sections in the following list. Nevertheless, for the sake of clarity, the minimum we would want to introduce to a project at this stage would be:

- Scope Change Management
    - Scope Change Request Forms
    - Scope Change Summary (probably a spreadsheet)

- Project governance tiers (described in the *Project initiation* section in *Chapter 1, Installing and Setting up Sure Step*)
- Budgeting tied to the Work Breakdown Structure (WBS)
- Time planning (tied to the WBS)
- Granular task management (tied to the WBS)

The Sure Step client defines and provides content for all **Cross Phase Processes** (activities) as shown in the following screenshot. Look into the client software to review the content and guidelines and decide what you will apply.

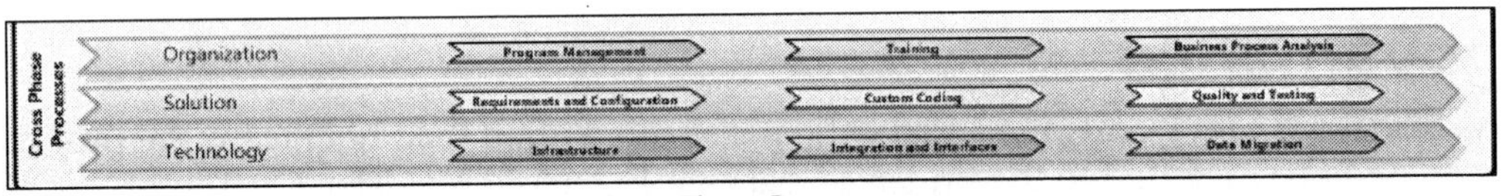

Cross Phase Processes

The Sure Step client defines and provides content for project management disciplines as shown in the following screenshot. Look into the client software to review the content and guidelines and decide what you will apply.

Project Management Library

The Sure Step client defines and provides content for organizational change management as shown in the following screenshot. Look into the client software to review the content and guidelines and decide what you will apply. Whereas all projects require Cross Phase activities and project management, only standard and enterprise projects need much consideration of the organizational change management content.

Organizational Change Management Library

Multi-consultant diagnostics

As projects evolve, it becomes more common to have multiple consultants working on a Diagnostic. This is desirable from several perspectives:

- Creating a broader team increases the bandwidth and reduces timescales
- Having multiple consultants enables the subject matter experts to engage their specialties

- Multiple team members enable peer reviews of the subject matter
- Having more than one person insures the project against consultants' unavailability

It is however undesirable if the consultants do not share their observations with each other, or fail to present them in a consistent manner. Having experienced this previously, we wanted to point out three obvious mitigations: set a document style and template before starting work, understand how several authors work will be combined together, and regularly review the output throughout the process.

A multi consultant diagnostic requires at least the following roles: planner (normally a project manager), the involvement of the senior sales team member, and a managing consultant. All should be parties to signing off the final draft before it is presented to the client.

Diagnostic review and Sign off

The Diagnostic outputs should be reviewed and signed off internally as discussed previously, before being introduced to the customer. It is a good practice to review the final draft with the customer's sponsor before it is presented to their wider project team.

Acquiring physical sign offs of a Diagnostic (or indeed any piece of paper implying responsibility within a project) can be a challenge. In the case of the Diagnostic, it is very important that unequivocal sign off has been provided by all of the key project stakeholders. Ideally, this will be a representative group including key users who are empowered on behalf of the end users.

One very common feature of signing off a Diagnostic is that it can be reviewed by quite a large audience and will need to pass through several—perhaps many, iterations of revision and review. In a larger organization, this can take months from completing the first draft. The importance of including detailed revision tracking of this document cannot be understated. We have found that keeping the marked up reviews of the drafts alongside the finished document in the repository can be very helpful to find out what changed, when, and why.

Once a Diagnostic has been finally signed and the Analysis phase has started, changes should be made via the scope change mechanism—not necessarily revising the Diagnostic output. However this is handled, it needs to be clearly communicated because the initial scope may form the basis of many scope change requests affecting time and budget later on.

Vertical markets

Vertical markets refer to specific industries with common functional requirements. These might include manufacturers, retailers, public sector companies, and many others. Within a vertical market, there tends to be several tiers of sub verticals. Consider just a few of the variants of manufacturing customers below:

Vertical	Subvertical	Sub-subvertical
Manufacturing	Process manufacturing	Life sciences
Manufacturing	Process manufacturing	Chemicals
Manufacturing	Process manufacturing	Food and beverage
Manufacturing	Discrete manufacturing	Building products
Manufacturing	Discrete manufacturing	Furniture
Manufacturing	Discrete manufacturing	Plant and machinery
Manufacturing	Hybrid manufacturing	Life sciences packaged drugs manufacturers

When operating in vertical markets, it is of course common to come across customers with similar needs. If you have previously implemented software into a similar company, the Diagnostic phase as well as the rest of the project tends to be much easier. It is of course necessary to be aware that two companies in the same sector may have quite different business processes. Nevertheless, deep industry knowledge would enable a consultant to quickly identify which of the common industry models do and do not apply. Working within verticals can enable fast understanding of a client's needs, supporting use of the Rapid project type, and the delivery of template projects. The increased **Time to Value (TtV)** and reduced risk is much favoured by experienced practitioners. It is a folly to think that having completed a project for one customer, it is now a vertical market; though, a true vertical market practice will understand all of the common business models in that market and create template solutions accordingly.

Third party products

The AX marketplace has matured in recent years, and now there are many readily available products to enhance the functionality and fit of the standard system.

Independent Software Vendors (ISVs), create solutions to enhance standard products. These can be very large solutions or tiny components.

Microsoft has an accreditation program for ISVs called the **Certified for Microsoft Dynamics (CfMD)** program. A product with CfMD accreditation has been reviewed to a certain set of quality and consistency standards and can be expected to have some longevity.

Adding one ISV solution to an AX system has been easy for some time, although the normal considerations for further bespoke development need to be considered carefully.

With AX 2012, it is now much easier and more common to combine multiple ISV solutions. It is incumbent on the partner to check the interoperability of combined solutions especially where they overlap modified functionality, such as pricing and inventory reservations.

Some common sources of ISV solutions are easily researched using Microsoft's Pinpoint website or looking at Microsoft conference materials—especially vendor listings from U.S. Convergence. There are also a number of common industry forums including Dynamics World, LinkedIn, and Mibuso.

Some of our favourite ISVs are:

AXtension®

AXtension is an ISV with CfMD enhancements for discrete and project manufacturers. AxTension ISVs also have some good generic content, such as a SharePoint integration.

The URL for this ISV is `www.axtension.com`.

AxPact Additions

A global organisation with members in most countries, AxPact has amassed a considerable catalogue of enhancements.

The URL for this ISV is `www.axpactadditions.com`.

BI4Dynamics

BI4Dynamics is a Business Intelligence provider with a neatly packaged Data Warehouse and accompanying set of OLAP cubes and Excel spreadsheets.

The URL for this ISV is `www.bi4dynamics.com`.

Atlas

Atlas is real-time, two-way integration software for Microsoft Dynamics AX and Microsoft Office. It allows you to build sophisticated reports and queries, as well allowing you to write-back into Microsoft Dynamics AX. This is all done through a simple, easy-to-use interface in combination with Microsoft Dynamics AX connector software that ensures the results are secure, accurate, and reliable. Atlas is used by organizations in all aspects of their daily operations and is commonly used during the implementation lifecycle and transitioning from one system to another.

To-Increase

To-Increase develops end-to-end solutions for construction, discrete manufacturing, distribution, food and beverage manufacturing, and retail and wholesale verticals, and reaches all industries with their business process modeling and business integration solutions.

The URL for this ISV is `www.to-increase.com`.

Dynamics Anywhere

Dynamics Anywhere is a company offering mobile solutions out of the box, such as warehousing, retail, field sales, and production. It is based on a powerful framework entirely integrated in Dynamics AX, offering partners and customer full flexibility to modify any of the solutions themselves.

The URL for this ISV is `www.dynamicsanywhere.com`.

Dynamics Software

Dynamics Software amplifies Dynamics AX by providing additional software for a number of areas including Service Management, Mobile Field Services, Maintenance Management, Warehouse Management, Graphical Planning and Scheduling, Dealer Management, Rental Management, and more.

Scalable ISV International

Scalable ISV International is an ISV and Dynamics AX Gold Partner since 1999. Scalable's suite of award-winning AX solutions substantially enhances the Dynamics AX Supply Chain Solution. Scalable's sophisticated suite of AX solutions are of particular benefit to Manufacturing (process and discrete), Distribution, Engineering, Mining and Mining Supply, as well as Commodities Trading.

The URL for this ISV is `www.scalable-data-systems.com`.

If you are interested in any of these vertical industries, you should contact a Scalable ISV Channel Manager to access webinars, white papers, and a wide selection of co-brandable brochure material. They would be happy to help you understand these solutions and their unique and robust value proposition.

Red Maple™

Another ISV with a large catalogue of solutions including Advanced Credit Cards™, Advanced Workflow™, Workflow Templates™, Advanced Trade & Pricing™, Advanced Commissions™, Advanced Budgeting™, Purchase Rebates™, Document Management™, Chargeback Claims™, and Warranty Management™.

The URL for this ISV is `www.redmaple.com`.

As good as third party products may be, their use should be tempered by the following questions:

- Are they supportable by the project team—is training required?
- Are they sustainable—what happens if the vendor has problems?
- Do they work together—do they overlap in their code footprint or purpose?
- Will the solution be upgradeable?
- Are the accompanying contracts acceptable?
- Are they affordable?
- Are they available for the version you intend to implement?
- Is the partner comfortable with the solution?
- It may at first seem that the partner's comfort with the solution is not tantamount, but we believe that it is very important to consider their experience. One partner may prefer a different approach based on their experience. For example, one partner may prefer a To-Increase solution for Discrete Manufacturing, and one may prefer an AxTension solution for Discrete Manufacturing. If the partner has training and experience with one product, that may well be the best product to choose when working with that partner.

Kick-offs

Sure Step identifies the need for, and provides some excellent content for kick-off and project summary meetings. These include the Diagnostic as a whole, as well as each of the Decision Accelerators independently, and the other project phases. Rather than simply following all of the Sure Step content and burning too much time in kick-off and wrap-up meetings, this is one area where we prefer to look at the Diagnostic as a whole and plan what kick-offs are required and who needs to attend them.

Summary

In this chapter, we reviewed the eight Decision Accelerators that might be included in a Diagnostic phase of a project managed using Sure Step. We considered when to use the various accelerators and that not all are necessary on every project, although some consideration of their content should always be made. For example, not undertaking a discrete scoping assessment would not mean a project has no scope. In practice, the Decision Accelerators should be combined to make a holistic Diagnostic offering to the customer.

We also considered an overlap with the sales activities—as the project may not yet be sold and overlap with the Analysis phase—as it is good to establish appropriate controls and disciplines as early as possible.

Finally, in this chapter we reviewed the availability of enhancement solutions, where to find them, and some of the considerations of using one or more of them on a project.

In the next chapter, we will cover planning the infrastructure to support Dynamics AX, including when you should begin the planning of infrastructure, choosing your team, and deciding on key technologies and roles.

3

Planning the Infrastructure to Support Dynamics AX

Dynamics AX 2012 is a complex enterprise product with multiple components, which have dependencies on several platform technologies. Even for a very small (20-30 user) installation, the AX components should be distributed across multiple servers (either physical or virtual), making the assessment and planning of infrastructure a very important task in every project. Even when considering an upgrade from a prior version of Dynamics AX or extending a current implementation, the existing infrastructure should be reviewed to ensure that it will continue to perform under the increased workload.

As this book is concerned with helping you implement a Dynamics AX 2012 project using Sure Step, this chapter will not focus on infrastructure sizing metrics or specific implementation designs. Instead, it will help you decide who to involve, and what needs to be considered in the planning processes by highlighting the key technological areas to look at when designing an infrastructure to support AX.

In this chapter, we will look at:

- When and how you should start planning infrastructure
- How to get the most out of your team by choosing people with the correct level of skill and experience for your project
- The key technologies and roles you must consider in order to achieve a successful AX implementation

When should you start planning infrastructure

Providing access to a working copy of AX at an early stage in the project has a number of benefits in building familiarity with the product in the customer's team, and demonstrating and testing standard functionality. The Hyper-V image that Microsoft makes available through customer and partner source is normally sufficient for this purpose and can be mounted on almost any virtualization platform with spare resource.

While the Microsoft image is excellent for Proof of Concept, familiarization, and demonstration purposes, as soon as the project team is ready to start configuring the actual system, you'll need to have an environment installed and configured that more closely resembles your live deployment. As such, we advise starting infrastructure planning activities early in the project, so that you know what environments you will deliver and when.

Choosing a team

Who will be involved in infrastructure planning depends on the size and reach of the project. For instance, a global project being rolled out in multiple countries will most certainly involve local teams in each location and require significant planning and coordination.

Smaller or single site deployments will not need as many people, but we still need to ensure we have the right skills and knowledge represented. In the rest of this chapter, we will touch on each of the platform products and AX roles and discuss how they affect infrastructure planning. This is designed to help you choose the right people to involve in the infrastructure planning phase and to provide some guidance as to what needs to be considered and discussed.

When deciding who to involve, make sure there is someone with sufficient knowledge of each product or role to ensure that each component is properly considered. In many cases, the partner will have one or more experts who they will want to involve in the planning. However, if we already have some of the components installed, or plan to use them for other applications besides Dynamics AX, for example a central SQL Server, then it won't be sufficient to just involve the person from the partner.

The investment in Dynamics AX is typically significant and the expectation is that the product will have a long life span. The infrastructure required to support AX should be viewed in the same way and should form a key part of the IT strategy. Avoid the temptation to view the Dynamics AX infrastructure separately from the core network, running on a few dedicated servers bought specifically for the project. When we've finished our project, AX will be an integral part of our business and will be entrenched in nearly every department in the business.

Planning and implementing the AX infrastructure will typically involve the customer's internal IT department or outsourced managed service provider. If IT also owns the Dynamics project, there is no conflict between departments and infrastructure planning and execution tends to be given as high a priority as other project tasks. If the Dynamics project is not owned by IT, it is very important to get their buy-in at an early stage, as they will need to work closely with the partner, internal project team, and users to deliver a fast and functional Dynamics AX implementation.

Finally, consider who will support the systems once the project is complete. Avoid waiting to engage support staff until the project is live. Involving them in the planning stages will make them better equipped to provide support post go-live, and their experience with existing systems and common problems may help you avoid some issues by engineering them out in the planning and design.

> **Make sure IT is on-board!**
>
> Involve IT from the initial planning of the project, and throughout the implementation. The cooperation of the team who provides and supports your infrastructure is critical to your project's success. Involve IT in your project meetings in order to include their input, and give them as much notice of new or changed requirements as possible. This will ensure that you receive the support you'll need from IT during go-live and in the "bedding in" period that follows.

Key technologies and roles to consider

Before starting to design our AX infrastructure, we need to establish how critical a system AX will be once it's live and what sort of uptime we need to provide. Agreeing this at the outset will help inform the decisions we make about high availability, disaster recovery, and so on, which in turn, will allow us to specify the hardware and software we require. It will also help us to determine the level of support the systems will need once they are live. Use the following to help start your discussions about how important system uptime will be to the business:

- How critical will AX be to the operation of the business? What would it cost the business if the system was not available for an hour or a day or a week? Also, consider both average and peak trading times when planning.
- If you were forced in to a DR (disaster recovery, discussed in detail below) scenario, what percentage of AX users would need to maintain access? How important would performance be during DR?
- How much data could you stand to lose if your database server was destroyed? 1 day, 1 hour, or less?
- Will AX be integrated with any other systems? How critical are those systems? Could they still function if AX was down? (Think process control systems, warehousing and dispatch, e-commerce systems, websites and POS).
- What are your hours of business? Does anyone *need* access to AX outside of these hours?

> **Be realistic!**
>
> Avoid allowing people to simply demand the system to be always available. 99.9 percent uptime with high performance comes at a very high price. Ensure you don't spend money unnecessarily or worse, sacrifice performance to meet an unnecessary uptime goal. No one will thank you for providing a system that is always available, but always slow!

High Availability and Disaster Recovery

Once we've determined the kind of uptime and performance we need to provide for AX, we can start to look at the technologies that could be used to deliver it. There are two common terms used when talking about keeping IT systems online and available to users, these are **High Availability** (**HA**) and **Disaster Recovery** (**DR**).

High Availability refers to technology intended to prevent live systems from going down in the first place. These include things like uninterruptable power supplies, which provides battery backup in the event of power failures, redundant components to mitigate server component failure, and **Redundant hard disk arrays (RAID)**, which provide redundancy (except for RAID 0) and performance benefits by spreading data and load over multiple disks so that if one fails, the system can carry on operating with no loss of data. Enterprise grade High Availability builds on these technologies to offer features aimed at trying to keep multiple servers online at once. For example, **Storage Area Networks (SANs)** move the hard disks out of individual servers into a shared system that can be accessed by multiple servers simultaneously, providing they have the correct configuration and technologies. This means that if server A fails, server B can take over its work as it can see server A's hard disks.

Disaster Recovery refers to the plans and systems we put in place to ensure that we can continue to operate in the event of a major system failure or physical disaster, like a fire that destroys the servers used to run the live systems.

High Availability technologies have evolved considerably as IT systems have become more important to businesses. Before technologies like virtualization and SANs became more affordable, true HA (High Availability) was really only a consideration for enterprise businesses. Historically, smaller installations used HA technologies in individual servers to try and minimize the risk of failure. Their High Availability strategy did not extend as far as trying to keep multiple servers running or providing real-time failover in the event that they did fail. This approach was fine when Dynamics AX ran on one or two servers, but AX 2012 has many roles which should be distributed across several servers. To keep an AX 2012 system fully online, the following roles, spread across multiple physical or virtual servers, need to be maintained:

- Active Directory Services
- SQL Server
- Dynamics AX **Application Object Server**
- SharePoint
- Workflow
- AIF
- Help
- Analysis Services (OLAP cubes that are used with in Business Intelligence)
- Reporting Services (SSRS, all AX documents and reports are delivered through Reporting Services)
- Other components used as part of your solution

With falling hardware costs, we now have several technologies available to us to provide highly available systems, even in smaller installations, which are explained in the following list:

- Data can be protected by RAID arrays within servers or in a SAN. When SANs are used in conjunction with Virtualization, it allows virtual servers running the AX roles discussed previously to be moved between different physical servers, with no noticeable downtime in the event that a physical server fails or during planned maintenance.
- The SQL Server can be protected using "failover clustering", which also relies on a SAN and multiple servers. This is discussed in more detail later.
- Full DR sites are increasingly common. This is effectively a second set of servers designed to provide the critical roles to avoid disruption to the company's operations. This DR site could be in another part of the building, at another site within the business, or at a shared third party data centre.

The exact implementation of High Availability and Disaster Recovery will depend on:

- The performance you need to provide
- The downtime your users will tolerate
- The physical design of your infrastructure (you may need to use different technologies when making services Highly Available across a wide area network than you would within the same data center)

The team you assemble to plan the infrastructure should be able to design a solution with the appropriate level of High Availability, based on the uptime and performance requirements and the technologies in use in the current infrastructure. In addition, the following points might be useful as a starting point for the HA discussion:

- **Virtualization**: If this incorporates a SAN to allow the **Virtual Machines** (**VMs**) to be moved between hosts, we immediately protect ourselves against physical hardware failure, providing there are sufficient free resources in the pool for the VMs to failover. As a rule, all AX components and dependent platform components can, and should be virtualized, except SQL Server which will be discussed later.
- **AOS Servers**: Consider whether you want to load balance the users across multiple servers. When clustered, AOS servers provide a measure of High Availability as when one server fails, users can re-connect to another by simply restarting the client. The main reason to cluster AX Object Servers is for scalability, so this will likely be used even if Virtualization is in place to provide the High Availability.

- **Critical Roles**: Not all roles have to have the same requirement for High Availability. Consider the Dynamics AX Help Server role; would it cause problems if the contextual help was offline for a day? Consider the same in DR. How important would it be to have access to the Business Intelligence OLAP Cubes and reports in DR? In which case, does **SQL Server Reporting Servers** (**SSRS**) or **SQL Server Analysis Services** (**SSAS**) need to be Highly Available? Bear in mind that SSRS is used for all reporting in AX 2012, including Delivery Notes, Invoices, and so on.
- **DR**: How far will your contingency plans go? Will there be a complete set of servers at the DR site configured to run all the AX roles in the event you need to failover, and how closely synchronised to LIVE will they be?

The database - Microsoft SQL Server

At the core of Dynamics AX, like all ERP systems, there is a database. AX 2012 supports the standard and enterprise editions of Microsoft SQL Server 2008 R2 and Microsoft SQL Server 2012.

Designing and sizing the database server is quite possibly, the most important and the most difficult part of the infrastructure design. Get it wrong, and the performance of AX will be severely compromised. The planning team should include an SQL Server expert who will lead the design process and define every part for the solution from disk arrays and CPUs, through to memory and clustering. It cannot be stressed enough how important a properly specified database server will be in ensuring that your AX solution performs the way you want.

Choosing your server

For a long time it was simple; Microsoft did not support Dynamics AX running against a virtual SQL Server and that was the end of the debate. Now virtual configurations are officially supported and this raises the question, "Should I virtualize my database server?" This very much depends on the size of the implementation and the level of HA required. The question can only really be answered by your infrastructure planning team after considering how AX will be used, the uptime required, and the infrastructure technologies already in place. To get the debate started, we offer the following advice:

- For smaller installations where AX will be the only or primary user of the SQL server and where High Availability is only provided through the live migration of virtual machines, it is reasonable to consider virtualizing the database server on condition that:
    - Adequate disk performance from the SAN can be guaranteed.

  - The virtual machine is given the highest priority, and in normal operation, it is run on a physical host with minimal demands from other VMs.
  - Adequate CPU cycles, memory, and network bandwidth are made available to the VM.

- In larger installations (above 50 users), or where other applications will make significant use of the database server, or where full failover clustering is required, SQL Server should be run on physical servers. In this scenario, SQL Server is likely to make use of all the resources of the physical server making the economies of resource sharing, one of the main arguments for virtualization, redundant in this case.
- In all cases, except where DR should provide identical performance to the live environment, virtualization can be used for the DR SQL Server.

Clustering: Active/Active versus Active/Passive

If we choose to use full failover clustering for the SQL server, we are faced with a choice: Do we try and maximize use of hardware by running Active/Active, or do we take safest and most highly preferred route by using Active/Passive? This is a debate you are likely to encounter, especially if you have followed the previous guidance and decided to use physical, not virtual, servers for SQL. When faced with the prospect of not fully utilising servers through virtualization, it is common for infrastructure teams to try and make use of the spare capacity through the use of Active/Active clustering. To briefly explain what these two options mean:

- In an Active/Active 2-node (server) cluster, both servers are performing live functions at all times. If the first node fails, the databases it was hosting are transferred to the second node. The second node is now doing its original work plus that of the first node. While this configuration provides the best performance in normal operation by utilizing the power of both servers for live applications, it suffers a performance hit in a failover situation.
- In an Active/Passive 2-node cluster, the second server is not used by any live applications in normal operation. Just as in Active/Active, if the first node fails, the databases it was hosting are transferred to the second node. But because the second node wasn't running any live applications, and providing it is the same specification as the first, there is no performance hit.

It is important to decide whether the hit in performance in a failover scenario is acceptable before deciding on which clustering option to choose. We would definitely recommend you to avoid installing multiple roles on the same node. For example, installing SQL Server as active on node one and passive on node two, and installing Exchange Server as active on node two and passive on node one should be avoided. Mixing roles like this, while technically possible, is not a good practice as both applications will fight for the same resources (that is, CPU time, memory, and disk access), and their coexistence can lead to complex technical problems that require significant time to resolve.

SQL Server edition

AX makes no specific demands of SQL Server that are not catered for by the Standard edition. In larger installations, the Enterprise edition provides support for additional memory (up to the OS limit rather than 64 GB) and additional CPUs (more than 4 sockets or 16 cores). In addition to the improved resource utilisation, the Enterprise edition offers asynchronous mirroring, which can be useful in provisioning WAN-based failover, and online indexing, which can improve uptime and performance in certain scenarios.

> **AX Support for Advanced Features**
>
> Note that not all of the advanced features of SQL Server Enterprise are supported by Dynamics AX. Unlike many applications which simply use SQL Server to host their database, AX interacts with its database at a deep level, creating and dropping fields and tables, and adjusting indexes through the application itself. As such, not every feature of SQL Server can be used by AX, and it is important to check the reasons for selecting the Enterprise edition are valid.

Application Object Server (AOS)

The **Application Object Server** (**AOS**) is responsible for running the application code that retrieves and processes data from the database before presenting it to the user through the client. The AOS is the middle portion of the three tiers that make up the Dynamics AX application architecture. A three-tier architecture means that the functionality of the application has been separated into three distinct parts or tiers, which are as follows:

- **Data Tier**: Provided by Microsoft SQL Server, the Data Tier is responsible for storing, indexing, and retrieving the data entered into Dynamics AX.

- **Application Tier**: Provided by the AOS, the Application Tier communicates with the data tier and is responsible for running the program logic that acts on the data, for example, running the code that generates a sales invoice. The AOS retrieves information from the Data Tier and passes back new or amended data to be stored. As the AOS servers run all the business logic, they, in combination with the Data Tier, are primarily responsible for AX performance.
- **Presentation Tier**: In the case of Dynamics AX, this can be provided by the AX Client (a program installed on a user's computer or a terminal server) or the Enterprise Portal (a web-based interface that runs in SharePoint). The Presentation Tier communicates with the Application Tier to allow data to be displayed, edited, and saved. As the business logic is run in the Application Tier, the performance of the Presentation Tier hardware has less of an impact on overall AX performance, although it should still be considered.

Now we know what role the AOS server performs we need to consider:

- how many of them we need (there must be a minimum of 1)
- how Highly Available they need to be
- how we will distribute the workload across them

The partner usually specifies the AOS server requirements based on their analysis of the activities they expect the users to perform, the frequency, volume and type of transactions, the other systems that will interact with AX, and the uptime requirement.

It is common for the AOS servers to be virtualized in live environments, and providing they are given sufficient resources, it is rare to experience performance problems directly attributable to the performance of the AOS. If you do choose to virtualize the AOS servers, monitor actual resource usage after go-live, and work with the infrastructure team to tune the virtual server specifications to meet the live workload.

Consider a Dedicated Batch Server

Before AX 2012, it was common for smaller installations to run on a single AOS server which handled clients and batch jobs. In our practical experience with AX 2012 in a live environment, performance and user experience is greatly improved by running all batch jobs on a separate AOS server that doesn't service client requests. This has the added benefit of providing an additional AOS server that could be used by clients in the event the primary AOS failed, improving HA.

Microsoft SQL Server Reporting Services (SSRS)

In the previous versions of Dynamics AX, reporting was handled using a reporting engine built into the core of the AX program. In AX 2012, this has been deprecated and replaced with integration to Microsoft's generic reporting engine, SSRS, which is part of the SQL Server product family.

SSRS handles all reporting output from AX. This includes listing reports like the trial balance, as well as document layouts, such as delivery notes and sales invoices. SSRS is also used to generate the charts and graphs used on the role center home pages.

Although SSRS is a standard feature of SQL Server, its implementation with AX is extended and uses .NET code to retrieve data from the database via the AOS servers rather than direct SQL queries. SSRS may already be used for internally developed reports or as part of another application; however, you should not plan to reuse that Reporting Services instance for AX.

SSRS can be installed on the same server as the main SQL Server database engine at no additional licence cost and in smaller installations, or in systems with very low reporting requirements; this is often the preferred approach. In larger installations where it is important that reporting demands do not affect the performance of the database server, it is a good practice to install the Reporting Services instance for AX on a separate server.

You should plan to provide at least one Reporting Services instance exclusively for use by AX. If high volumes of reporting are expected, consider running multiple SSRS instances on separate servers. Remember, each SSRS installation on a separate server requires an SQL Server license, however, you do not have to match editions, for example, the main database server could use Enterprise and the reporting servers could use Standard.

If the generation of reports or layouts is critical to live operation, ensure that the SSRS server is highly available by running it on a virtual machine capable of failing over in the event of hardware failure.

Microsoft SQL Server Analysis Services (SSAS)

Analysis Services, like Reporting Services is another standard component of SQL Server and is used to facilitate data analysis and reporting using a technology called **Online Analytical Processing** (**OLAP**). It is used to build and process the standard OLAP cubes which ship with Dynamics AX. These cubes provide segmented views of Dynamics AX data to allow rapid aggregation and analysis of values split by different dimensions, for example, Sales by Customer by Month. Many of the charts and graphs on the AX role centers draw their data from the OLAP cubes.

Unlike Reporting Services, SSAS retrieves its data directly from the AX database and does not send any requests via the AOS servers. It is not necessary to run a separate instance of SSAS for AX unless you need to isolate it for performance reasons. Security roles built into Analysis Services allow granular control of access to data and views on a per cube basis, so it is not necessary to separate it for security purposes.

SSAS can be installed on the same server as the main SQL Server database engine at no additional license cost. As Analysis Servers supports failover clustering, it is not uncommon, in larger installations, to install the SSAS cluster on the physical hardware as the main SQL cluster to take advantage of the processing power of what would have been the passive node during normal operation. In a failover scenario, Analysis Services can be stopped or given a lower priority to ensure that the database server gets the resources it needs; however, a scenario where both roles run on the same node should be taken into account during the server sizing.

You should plan to provide at least one instance of SSAS, typically on the same server as the main database engine. If OLAP usage is predicted to be high, consider implementing a failover cluster for the database engine and installing SSAS on the passive node. As with Reporting Services, each installation on a separate server requires an SQL Server license, but you do not have to match editions unless the installations are part of the same cluster.

SharePoint and Search Server

Dynamics AX has two Presentation Tier technologies: the AX client, a traditional Windows application, and the Enterprise Portal, a web-based interface. The Enterprise Portal is built on the Microsoft SharePoint 2010 platform and requires a dedicated site within a SharePoint installation to run. The Enterprise Portal is also responsible for displaying the role center home pages displayed in AX and storing the document templates used by the Microsoft Word and Excel add-ins.

Microsoft Search Server is another product in the SharePoint family and is used to provide rapid searching of SharePoint content and external data sources. A provider installed as part of the AX setup routine allows Search Server to index AX data, and allows you to include results from AX in searches performed in SharePoint.

An important question to consider when planning the SharePoint and Search Server requirements for AX is "Does this need to form a part of a wider SharePoint strategy?" By this we mean, do you currently run, or do you plan to run SharePoint as an application in its own right for intranet and document management purposes? If the answers is yes and the edition you run is 2010, then you can consider deploying Enterprise Portal as a site within that SharePoint farm. This will require cooperation between the AX partner and the team responsible for SharePoint, as the integration of an Enterprise Portal site into an existing SharePoint environment can be complicated and requires careful planning and installation.

If there is no existing installation or plans to deploy SharePoint for anything other than Enterprise Portal, a single virtual server running SharePoint Foundation Server 2010, a free edition of SharePoint, and Search Server Express 2010, also free, can be sufficient to run the Enterprise Portal and Search components of AX, depending on how heavily Enterprise Portal will be used. Both SharePoint and Search Server rely on Microsoft **Internet Information Services 7** (**IIS 7**, the web server that ships as a part of Windows 2008). IIS 7 is also required for the AX help server role, and it is common to install these roles on the same server.

Microsoft Lync

More of a consideration than a requirement, Microsoft Lync is the new name for Microsoft Office Communications Server, Microsoft's unified communications platform. Lync provides voice, video, and instant messenger communications internally and externally. Lync can act as a VoIP telephone system, or can be integrated with third party systems to add unified communications functionality to an existing phone system. The Lync client is fully integrated into Microsoft Office and provides presence information and instant communication features, when interacting with contacts in Microsoft Office products.

Dynamics AX 2012 includes a Lync connector, which extends these features to the AX client, allowing users to view presence information and initiate phone calls, e-mails, and instant message conversations from AX.

If Lync is already installed, or is planned for installation in the future, make sure the Lync team are aware of the AX project and ensure that the Lync integration is enabled in the configuration when AX is installed.

Active Directory

Dynamics AX 2012 does not store separate usernames and passwords to manage user access. Instead, it uses **Active Directory** (**AD**) and stores a mapping between an AX user and an AD user account. When a user runs the AX client, details of the User Credentials (**SID**) are passed to AX, which matches them to the equivalent AX user account. This is then used to grant specific permissions within the application. While this provides a seamless logon experience for the user and improves the security of AX, it does create the following considerations for the infrastructure planning team which they may not have experienced with previous software products:

- The AX client and AX server roles can only be installed on domain joined computers and servers.
- There is no way to log in to AX other than to have an AX user account linked to an AD user.
- The first user to run the AX client after installation will be automatically mapped to the Admin user account in AX. Consider making sure that this is done using the domain administrator account or a new dedicated AX administrator account created in AD. *DO NOT* try logging in with local accounts.
- AX needs to be installed on servers in the same Active Directory forest that will be used for live operation; *do not* install AX in an isolated forest with a view to migrating it before go-live.
- Follow the instructions in the installation guide and create domain accounts for all AX and platform product services to run under.

No changes or extensions to the Active Directory schema are made by AX as the integration is purely one-way, that is, AX reading AD.

Dynamics AX Client and Office Add-in

The Dynamics AX client is a Windows application that connects to the AOS servers to provide users with access to the AX system. It is the most commonly used method of access for regular users of AX. When designing our AX infrastructure, it is important to consider how the AX client will be deployed to users taking into account requirements for communication between the AOS servers and the client.

As most of the data access and processing is taken care of by the SQL Server and AOS servers, the hardware requirements for the AX client are similar to a Microsoft Office user. What the client needs more than resources on the local machine, is a fast (low latency) connection to the AOS servers. This presents little difficulty when deploying the client within the confines of a **local area network** (**LAN**), but presents more of a challenge when rolling AX out to remote users or other sites over a **wide area network** (**WAN**). Where WAN access is required, Windows Remote Desktop Services or Citrix are often used to deploy either the AX application or a whole desktop to remote users. This is a very common scenario and AX 2012 introduced new features specifically designed to improve the user experience when the AX client is deployed as a remote application. The most notable feature is the ability to send data from AX to the user's local copy of Excel, rather than the one installed on the server.

How the AX client is deployed to your users will very much depend on where they are, what hardware and operating systems they currently use, and how IT wants to deploy and manage applications. You may also find it useful to take the following into account:

- The AX client requires a minimum of Windows Vista Business and *WILL NOT* run on Windows XP.
- If users run all their other applications locally, wherever practically possible, deploy the AX client locally too. Having one application running remotely and all others locally, can be confusing to users and can create issues when working with file paths and printers.
- What other applications will AX need to communicate or interface with, for example Microsoft Outlook or client side **computer telephony integration** (**CTI**)? The limitations of these applications may dictate where the AX client is best deployed.
- The AX client does not need a high-bandwidth connection to the AOS servers, but it does need low latency. 4 ms or less is required for a fast and stable connection. If this cannot be provided over a WAN, consider using Remote Desktop Services or Citrix to provision access to the client.
- The client has been optimized to work with Windows Aero themes in Windows 7 and Windows Server 2008. Installing the Windows Experience Pack on servers and enabling an Aero-based theme on workstations will create the best user experience.

- AX forms and list pages contain a lot of information. To avoid lots of scrolling, consider providing heavy AX users with wide screen monitors capable of a reasonably high resolution. Having a standard resolution common to all users can help when designing custom forms and interfaces later in the project, but it is not essential. Some power users may benefit from having more than one display giving them even more room to work.

Microsoft introduced a new client-side feature in AX 2012 called the Microsoft Office Add-in. This Add-in works with Office 2007 and 2010, and adds a new ribbon to Word and Excel. The Add-in allows users to access data from AX and embed it in spreadsheets or documents. The Office Add-in requires the AX client and a reliable and fast connection to the AOS server. Whatever method is chosen for deploying the AX client, the same method should be chosen for the Office Add-in.

Environments

In *Chapter 4, Installing the Dynamics AX Environment*, we will look at installing, configuring, and managing our AX environments for the early stages of the project right through to go-live. In this chapter, we are more concerned with how many environments we will have, and what infrastructure we need to provide.

Start by planning your LIVE environment. Using the guidance in this chapter, your infrastructure planning team should have settled on a design for your live AX environment taking account of High Availability, Disaster Recovery, and performance. Now it's time to plan the non-live environments that will be used for development, testing, and training. The number of non-live environments will vary based on each customer's requirements. A typical implementation would include two of the following environments as a minimum:

LIVE (also called Production) environment

The main focus of this chapter, the Live environment, should be designed to provide the performance and uptime required in day-to-day operation. Live AX roles should be separated across multiple servers, and should be backed up in accordance with the backup and Disaster Recovery strategy.

PRE-LIVE or UAT (User Acceptance Testing) environment

An environment that should closely mirror LIVE, the PRE-LIVE environment, should be used to test how modifications to the application, or changes to the configuration will affect the live system when deployed. This environment is also used heavily in the months following go-live, when users want to experiment or try procedures in a test environment before doing them in LIVE.

From an infrastructure planning perspective, we need to decide how closely this environment should mirror LIVE, for example, should the AX roles be split across the same number of servers as in LIVE so that testing is performed on as close a mirror of LIVE as possible? In larger deployments, especially those with multiple AOS servers, this is certainly recommended.

Separate virtual servers should be used to replicate the LIVE servers, and the PRE-LIVE database should be installed on the LIVE database server wherever possible so that performance can be accurately assessed.

TEST environment

A TEST environment is used to deliver software modifications from development for the first pass of testing. This environment differs from PRE-LIVE in the sense that the modifications delivered to TEST are far more likely to contain bugs and issues and will require further development before being considered ready for LIVE. Once a modification has passed testing in TEST, it should be moved to PRE-LIVE to simulate how it will affect LIVE when deployed, and for final user training and testing.

As TEST is the first point of software delivery from development, it very quickly falls out of sync with the LIVE environment and thus, becomes unsuitable for user acceptance testing and training. Hence, there is the requirement to maintain a separate PRE-LIVE environment.

As TEST is only used to provide an environment for functional testing, there is no requirement to provide the same level of performance or role separation provided in LIVE or PRE-LIVE. Dynamics AX 2012 has a single server install option designed expressly for building environments like this. This option will install all AX roles and required platform products on a single server. The only change you may wish to make to the single server install is to place the database on another server, which already has SQL Server installed rather than licensing another instance just for TEST.

Development (DEV environment)

A DEV environment should be considered on projects where personnel on the customer's side will undertake development work as well as the partner. In this case, having an environment dedicated to development is essential if you want to leave TEST and PRE-LIVE clear for users' testing and training.

Just like TEST, the DEV environment can be installed on a single server with the potential to offload the SQL Server roles to save on licensing.

Real-world example

The following is an example of a real infrastructure design for a 250-user AX 2012 installation that went live in April 2012. It was written after completing the infrastructure planning activities discussed earlier. Note this is *NOT* a firm hardware or network design, but a list of requirements the AX project had for infrastructure.

Extract from a real project's infrastructure planning document: The following table shows the physical and virtual server requirements for the four proposed environments, plus Disaster Recovery. In planning, designing, and operating the virtualization environment, it is assumed that priority will be given to the LIVE servers ensuring that they always have access to their required resources.

Although Microsoft SQL Server is supported in a virtualized configuration, we recommend it to be run on physical servers to optimize performance and throughput. There have been reports of performance problems from other AX 2012 users who have opted to virtualize the SQL; so we recommend that the SQL Server remain physical, at least initially.

CPU cores in the virtualization hosts and the **database** (**DB**) servers should be the "current fast CPU". There are no specific requirements in terms of clock speeds and cores, so you should be guided by your hardware vendors as the best value/performance chip currently available.

Environment	Live			UAT (Pre-Live)			Test			Development			Disaster Recovery[4]		
Virtual Servers															
Server Role	Cores	RAM	HDD	Cores	RAM	HDD	Cores	RAM	HDD	Cores	RAM	HDD	Cores	RAM	HDD
Application Server AOS - 1	2	8 GB	60 GB	4	16 GB	60 GB	2	16 GB	500 GB[1]	4	16 GB	500 GB1	4	8 GB	60 GB
Application Server AOS - 2	2	8 GB	60 GB	-	-	-	-	-	-	-	-	-	-	-	-

Environment	Live			UAT (Pre-Live)			Test			Development			Disaster Recovery[4]		
Virtual Servers															
Server Role	Cores	RAM	HDD	Cores	RAM	HDD	Cores	RAM	HDD	Cores	RAM	HDD	Cores	RAM	HDD
Application Server AOS - 3	2	8 GB	60 GB	-	-	-	-	-	-	-	-	-	-	-	-
Application Server AOS - 4	2	8 GB	60 GB	-	-	-	-	-	-	-	-	-	-	-	-
Web Server IIS, SharePoint[2]	4	12 GB	60 GB	2	8 GB	60 GB	-	-	-	-	-	-	2	8 GB	60 GB
Reporting Server SSRS	2	16 GB	60 GB	2	8 GB	60 GB	-	-	-	-	-	-	2	8 GB	60 GB
Physical Servers															
Database[5] Server - Node 1 SQL, SSAS	2 x 4 Core	64 GB	3	-	-	-	-	-	-	-	-	-	4	32 GB	3
Database Server - Node 2 SQL, SSAS	2 x 4 Core	64 GB	3	-	-	-	-	-	-	-	-	-	-	-	-

The key information that can be taken from the previous table is outlined as follows:

1. As this environment will use a local SQL instance rather than the central cluster, the hard disk requirement of 500 GB is an estimate of the space required to hold the Windows OS, all required AX and SQL components, and a copy of the database. The full 500 GB will not be required initially; however, as the live database grows, the additional space will be required in order to load a copy on the test and development environments.
2. Refers to the initial deployment of SharePoint Foundation Server 2010, which will be used to support Dynamics AX Enterprise Portal in April 2012. It is envisaged that long-term the SharePoint requirements will be handled by a separate SharePoint farm and thus, the resource requirements of this server will be reduced.
3. The following only covers Dynamics AX's SQL Server requirements. If a single SQL server is to be used for the whole enterprise including applications other than AX, the requirements for all other SQL-based applications you plan to run will need to be taken into account.

   The following disk requirements are derived by performance requirements rather than storage space; however, as the DB server will be used to power both the LIVE and UAT environments, the storage capacity of 1,168 GB does not seem unreasonable for two copies of an AX database over five years. The biggest unknown in this area is the volume of documents (files) to be stored in the AX DB. Taking a view based on the amount of data held in the previous system's document store may help in sizing this requirement.

All disks used in the SQL Server and its SAN arrays should be SAS 3 15000 rpm.

Disk	Disk Requirements
OS	2 x 146 GB RAID 1 (local to server)
Data Array	16 x 146 GB RAID 10 (SAN Array)—1,168 GB capacity
Log Array	4 x 146 GB RAID 10 (SAN Array)—292 GB capacity
Temp DB Array	4 x 146 GB RAID 10 (SAN Array)—292 GB capacity
Quorum Array	2 x 146 GB RAID 1 (SAN Array)

4. Assumes a permanent DR environment is set up and configured at the DR location. If the DR strategy is to fail VM's over from the live site to the DR location, the DR environment can be removed from scope.
5. In DR, the SQL Server could be virtualized accepting that performance may be substantially reduced.

Summary

At the end of the infrastructure planning phase, you should have:

- Identified the necessary personnel you need to engage
- Held a roundtable meeting with all involved parties to discuss the project and establish the infrastructure requirements
- Established how critical AX and its various roles are to the business, and what sort of uptime needs to be provided
- Established how many environments you will need to provide
- Produced an infrastructure requirement similar to the example shown previously

The performance of your Live AX system will be significantly impacted by your infrastructure; so it is imperative that you spend the time and effort required to get a hardware design appropriate to your requirements for High Availability and performance. Engaging the right skills at an early stage will ensure this time and effort is well spent and will give you the best possible chance of success.

Now that we have discussed the importance of infrastructure planning, we are ready to move on to the installation of the Dynamics AX Environments. In the next chapter, we will be exploring which environment to provide access to and when, and also cover the key components of an AX installation.

4

Installing the Dynamics AX Environments

In the previous chapter, we discussed building a team to design and implement the infrastructure required to support the Dynamics AX infrastructure. In this chapter, we will focus on the installation and environment management process.

As this book's primary purpose is to help you plan, manage, and execute a successful Dynamics AX 2012 deployment end-to-end using the Sure Step 2012 methodology, we will not focus on the individual steps required to install each component and role. Instead, this chapter serves to highlight the key considerations and decisions that need to be made during installation, and will try to guide your deployment and ensure you provision the right environments at the right time.

For detailed instructions on how to install Dynamics AX 2012, please refer to the installation guide available on the product release download page in Customer and Partner Source, or the Microsoft training course MB6-872: Microsoft Dynamics AX 2012 Installation and Configuration, available to all customers and partners with active support plans.

This chapter will discuss the following:

- When to install AX Environments
- Installing AX
- Installing other environments

Getting started

As discussed in *Chapter 3, Planning the Infrastructure to Support Dynamics AX*, providing access to an AX environment at an early stage in the project is often beneficial as it allows both consultants and customers to start interacting with the software, demonstrating features, and testing ideas and theories. As we will see in the later chapters, there is a considerable amount of configuration and data setup required after AX has been installed before it is possible to process transactions. As such, early access is often best achieved by downloading and mounting the demonstration virtual machine, created by Microsoft. This image contains a fully configured, multi-company, and multi-national implementation of Dynamics AX including demo data, and can be used almost immediately after installation. The virtual machine is provided in Hyper-V format, but can be converted using tools such as VMware vCenter Converter, to run on other virtualization platforms. The server contains a Single Server installation of all the AX roles, as well as acting as a domain controller for the Contoso domain. Here are some tips for getting the Microsoft Demonstration Virtual Machine up and running for your project:

- **Download the image as soon as you can**: For customers, this is immediately after you receive your license and gain access to Customer Source. Partners should already have access via Partner Source. Do this as soon as it is practically possible—usually as soon as the decision to purchase AX has been made, normally at the start of the diagnostic.
- **Prioritize performance over High Availability**: As this machine will only be used for demos, testing, and prototyping, and will not contain any LIVE configuration that will need to be kept, it is best to prioritize performance over High Availability.
- **Provide as much RAM as you can**: In addition to acting as an Active Directory Domain Controller, the virtual machine is also running SQL Server, IIS, SharePoint Foundation Server, Search Server, the AOS Service, Remote Desktop Services, the AX client, and Office 2010. A minimum of 4 GB of RAM, but preferably 8 GB or more is required to make the server run smoothly. CPU time is also important, but more RAM usually makes the biggest difference to performance. Consider buying a high performance workstation to run the virtual machine on. As HA is unimportant, a workstation with a quad-core CPU, 8 GB of RAM, and a 128 GB **Solid State Drive** (**SSD**) drive makes an ideal platform on which to mount the image.
- **Do not try and join the virtual machine to your own domain or change the IP address of its internal network adapter**: Follow the setup guidelines that come with the image and don't be tempted to spend time integrating it into your network environment. Get as far as assigning it an IP address in your LAN so that you can access it with the Remote Desktop client and stop there.

- **Use the built-in roles**: The Contoso company comes preconfigured with Active Directory accounts for over 50 Contoso employees. The documentation provided with the VM explains what role each user is assigned to. Try logging in as different users to experience AX in their role. Do this before trying to set up your own accounts.
- **Don't be tempted to use the AX installation on the virtual machine as a starting point for your own configuration**: Do not start creating companies and configurations with the expectation that they can be exported and imported into LIVE later. While it is technically possible, moving data between environments has become a lot more complicated in AX 2012; the techniques and methods that may have worked with previous AX versions, no longer apply. When you are ready to start configuring, you are ready for your own environments.

> **You only get one chance to make a first impression!**
>
> Exposing the users to the system early in the project is usually beneficial, especially if it includes demos of impressive and potentially time-saving features. The fully configured Contoso system with its graphical role centers looks great and often generates considerable enthusiasm for AX and thus, the project. However, if the VM runs slowly because it hasn't got enough resources, they could end up with a negative view. Remember how important user buy-in is to the success of a project, and make sure your demo environment is impressive before letting the users loose! It is also a good idea to provide end users with a few scripts to try out to better demonstrate the powers of AX, rather than simply letting them click on various functions. Data and application objects (that is, forms) are cached on first access in AX, so it may be worth running through these scripts before passing over to end users to give the best impression of performance.

When to install your AX environments

Having provisioned a demo environment to allow the project initiation and diagnostic activities to get underway, it's time for the infrastructure team to start planning the installations within the customer's domain including the environment that will eventually become LIVE.

During infrastructure planning, we should have decided how many environments we need to provide, what servers the roles will be separated across, and what changes need to be made to the existing infrastructure. In most cases, additional hardware will be purchased to support the AX deployment and here comes the dilemma: If your project isn't scheduled to go-live for 18 months, should you delay buying the LIVE hardware until closer to the go-live date? Consider that servers come with a three-year warranty as standard, half the warranty period will have elapsed before you start using the hardware in production. It may make sense to delay the hardware purchase, but *NOT* if it will delay the creation of your environments.

If virtualization is going to be used, it becomes very simple for us to build the servers and install the environments required for our project without the new hardware, provided there is some capacity on the existing infrastructure. These servers can be configured with the correct names, IP addresses, roles, and service accounts, and when the additional hardware is installed, they will be migrated across to run in production with more resources. What this enables us to do, provided we have enough capacity, is to abstract the environment creation from the installation of hardware and potentially avoid one of the most common delays in a project—infrastructure not being ready on time.

Although virtualization allows us to run without our full production hardware, this doesn't mean it can be left until the last minute. Exactly when you'll need to make sure the VMs are running on their production hardware will depend on the project schedule, size of deployment, and amount of changes being made to the existing infrastructure. As a rule, it is a good practice to have the LIVE environment running on the production hardware 2-3 months prior to go-live. Wherever possible and certainly in larger deployments, the **User Acceptance Testing** (**UAT**) phase of deployment should be done on the production hardware to give an indication of how AX will perform when LIVE. Remember, UAT is not just about testing the business logic, custom developments, and configuration of Dynamics AX; it's a test of the server infrastructure and client environments as well. Better to iron out any problems during UAT than after go-live!

In summary, you should look to start provisioning your AX environments as early in the project as is practical. No configuration can take place until this is done and while the configuration workshops might appear some way off, there is nothing to lose by having the environments ready early. It also gives you time to deal with any issues you encounter during installation.

> While provisioning the environments as early as possible is desirable in all projects, it is essential in Agile projects. The Agile approach plans activities on a daily basis and seeks to start configuration and deployment activities at the beginning of the project at the same time as Diagnostic and Analysis. An Agile project will need at least a proper environment suitable for configuration work, typically no later than two weeks after project initiation.

Installing AX

The remainder of this chapter will focus on components that need to be installed to deliver our AX environments. For the purpose of this book, we will assume we are creating four environments, namely LIVE, PRE-LIVE, TEST, and DEV. We will start by discussing the order in which these should be installed.

Build order

In previous versions of AX, the application code and data were kept separately; the application was made up of files stored in a shared folder and the data was stored in the SQL Server database. Also, the data in each company was separated at kernel level and thus, could almost be thought of as separate databases.

> **AX2012 R2 changes**
>
> AX 2012 R2, released in December 2012, changes the application storage once again, moving the application code into a database separate from the data. This now means we have three SQL databases, for Data, Application, and Baseline.

Because of this, it was common to create a base configuration company (that would become the live company(s)), and use the company copy feature to create test and training companies.

Moving code and data between environments was relatively easy, and each partner would have developed their own techniques for managing this process.

In AX 2012, code has been moved from the file system into the same SQL database used to store the data. Also, new intercompany functionality in AX 2012 combined with new methods of sharing data across multiple companies, means that you can no longer have test companies safely in your LIVE environment. It also means that when code is moved between environments, more care should be taken.

Without getting into deep technical detail, AX 2012 requires that one environment be treated as the object master and thus, be responsible for assigning definitive object IDs when developing. Logically, this must be the LIVE environment, and so it is advisable to start by creating the LIVE environment when installing AX 2012. After that the order doesn't really matter, as long as the environments are created from the live model store/database. From this point, you need to maintain strict procedures for managing updates between environments.

Service accounts and admin rights

Before starting the installation, ensure that you have adequate permissions and a series of service accounts with the correct permissions. Full details of the service accounts required can be found in the installation guide provided by Microsoft.

DO NOT be tempted to use your own account, or worse, the administrator account during the installation and plan to swap to proper service accounts later. This could have many consequences and may end up destabilising the environments you've built. Unless explicitly stated in the installation guide, avoid using local or network service accounts.

The following is an example of the user accounts for services you will need to create. Typically, the same service accounts are used for all environments although separate sets of accounts for LIVE and non-LIVE environments can be used if security is a major concern. Note that when using different service accounts for different environments, testing of integrations and file share access in PRE-LIVE does not represent a full and fair test of functionality, as the credentials used in LIVE will be different.

User ID	Usage
SVC-DAX-BC	AX Business Connector proxy account
SVC-DAX-WF	AX Workflow system account
SVC-DAX-AOS	AX Application Server service account
SVC-SQL-SSAS	SQL Analysis Server account
SVC-SQL-SSRS	SQL Reporting Services account
SVC-SQL-SSAG	SQL Server Agent account
SVC-SQL-SSDB	SQL Server Service account

> The installation guide suggests creating another account for Search Server, but then later advises you to use the Business Connector account.

Checking the basics

Before installing any AX roles, it is important to make sure that the underlying server operating systems are installed, configured, and updated correctly. This should be a standard procedure for the infrastructure team, but we've seen hours of time lost to tracking down problems with data or currency logic, only to discover that the server, which the SQL Server is running on, has been set to the wrong locale. Consider the following when starting your installation:

- Make sure you are using a supported operating system. Check the current Microsoft documentation to find out. If you install AX on an unsupported OS and have problems later, Microsoft will not provide support.
- Check if the regional settings are configured appropriately for your region. AX uses the Windows regional settings to determine how to display dates, currencies, and amounts. Make sure these are set correctly *BEFORE* installing prerequisites like SQL Server.
- Run Windows Update and make sure the server is fully patched and up-to-date before starting your installation. If the AX prerequisites checker installs more components, for example, .Net 4.0, then drop out of setup before installing the roles, and run Windows Update again to make sure all new components have been updated as well.

SQL Server and the database role

AX has many prerequisites that must be met to complete a full installation, but the most fundamental is the database server and role. Without this, the Application Object Server role cannot be installed.

We will not discuss how to install and configure SQL Server in the book, except to highlight the following:

- Make sure SQL Server is installed and configured by someone with good product knowledge and experience. There is more to installing a high performing and reliable SQL Server than simply completing the installation routine.
- Ensure database files, logs, and TempDB are located on separate arrays, or LUNs in the case of shared array SANs. Change the default paths in SQL Server so that all new database files are created in the correct locations.
- Ensure that TempDB has been split, one file per CPU core.
- Ensure that TCP has been enabled as a communication protocol.

Once you have a fully installed and configured instance of SQL Server, run the Dynamics AX setup program on the SQL Server and install the database server role. Refer to the installation guide for detailed instructions.

Decide on a logical and clear naming convention and stick to it. For instance, if our company was called Contoso, consider: CTO_DAX6_LIVE and CTO_DAX6_LIVE_BL (for the baseline DB). CTO is a prefix derived from the name Contoso and is used to identify the organization. The baseline database is used when performing version or service pack upgrades and major code installs, and as such, each environment should have its own baseline DB even though AX gives you the ability to share a baseline between multiple environments.

During installation, the setup wizard offers a choice of model to import in addition to foundation. The upgrade layers are only relevant if you are upgrading from a previous version, and so can be ignored if you are implementing Dynamics AX 2012 from scratch. The other models (Process, Project Management, and Retail) are solutions that Microsoft has acquired and added into the core product. The decision as to which optional models to install will probably be made by the partner early in the diagnostic stage. It is important to make this decision before installing the LIVE environment, as adding the model later, while technically possible, will almost certainly involve more work and could break configuration and development work completed before the model was added. The label files are contained in separate models, so it is important to select the label model for each core model you choose.

Application Object Server

Installing the AOS is relatively straight forward and is comprehensively covered in the installation guide. Just like with databases, it's important to establish a naming convention for the AOS servers bearing in mind that it's possible to install multiple AOS instances on a single server. Following the example we used for databases, the AOS instances might be called: CTO_DAX6_LIVE_AOS1, CTO_DAX6_LIVE_AOS2, and so on.

In our four environment example scenario, we will have three LIVE AOS servers. AOS - 1 and AOS - 2 will be placed in a load balanced cluster and AOS - 3 will be configured as a dedicated batch server. All these options are set in the Server Configuration form in **Administration** | **Setup** once you have logged into AX using the client, so we don't need to concern ourselves with it during installation. Our only task is to run the setup routine on all three servers to create the LIVE instances of AX.

> **AX Client on Object Servers**
>
> While it's not strictly necessary to install the AX client or other client components on the AOS servers, we have encountered issues, particularly when applying Cumulative Updates, with the setup routine not recognizing installed components. Installing the client overcomes this and ensures all components are updated. It is also useful when logging into AX for the first time, and for administering the system before your LIVE client environments are fully configured.

Web-based AX Components

As discussed in *Chapter 3, Planning the Infrastructure to Support Dynamics AX*, it is not uncommon to install all the web-based AX components on a single server. This server will have a long list of prerequisites, all of which will be identified by the prerequisite check in the installation routine.

In our example deployment, we are assuming that a new installation of SharePoint Foundation Server will be used and thus, everything will be installed and configured specifically for AX on a single server. If you plan to integrate Enterprise Portal into an existing SharePoint 2010 installation, you will need to involve your SharePoint team and an Enterprise Portal expert from the partner to make sure the installation is performed correctly. The installation of Enterprise Portal has been known to cause issues when deployed into an existing LIVE SharePoint environment; so extra care should be taken.

Once you've completed the installation of the prerequisites, a single pass through the installation processes is all that's required to install Enterprise Portal, Search Server, and Help Server. Again, refer to the installation guide for detailed instructions, but in particular, note:

- The name you choose for the web components server must not contain any special characters, such as an _ (underscore), which are not part of the valid DNS standard. A - (hyphen) is acceptable.
- Create a separate website in IIS for the Help Server, and edit its binding to use a port other than 80. The Setup Wizard cannot cope with SharePoint and the Help Server being bound to the same port. It is much easier to reconfigure Help Server than it is to change SharePoint's default port assignment.

After the installation is complete, there are some important post-installation activities listed in the guide that you must complete. One of the most important and often overlooked points is granting AX users access to the SharePoint site. One of the most common complaints post go-live is users saying they don't have access to AX, and they get an access denied message. When the support team checks, they can see the user in the online users' list and say "You must be mistaken". What the user is actually seeing is a page from SharePoint as the AX client tried to access their default role center and found that they didn't have permission to access the page or site. The simplest way to solve this is to create an Active Directory group called Dynamics AX Users or something similar. Grant SharePoint access to this group and place all users who should have access to AX in it. The group can also be used to grant permission of file shares and folders that AX users might need access to while running the application. Consider creating multiple groups to assign users to different roles in SharePoint. For example, users who will edit and create role centers will need administrative access and could be placed in an AXSPAdmins group.

SQL Server Reporting Services

In our scenario, we have chosen to separate SSRS from the main SQL server cluster and install it on a separate virtual machine. Again, we won't focus on the individual steps required to install SSRS, as the AX installation guide contains detailed instructions on which service accounts to use and how to configure SSRS.

SSRS uses an SQL database to store configuration and report metadata. Do not confuse this with the AX database (known as the transactional database) it is reporting on. You can choose to locate this database on the primary SQL Server, or if you wish to keep it separate, install the database engine as well as Reporting Services on the SSRS server. In keeping with our naming convention, the database would be called CTO_SSRS_LIVE.

Once you have installed Reporting Services, make sure you follow the steps in the Dynamics AX guide carefully as it contains important information about security configurations without which, it will be impossible to deploy or access reports.

Once all the prerequisites are installed and the Reporting Services instance is properly configured, run the Dynamics AX 2012 setup and install the reporting role. During installation, the wizard will ask if you want to deploy the reports as part of setup; typically, we would advise saying yes at this point. Setup will eventually launch a command prompt style window running PowerShell. This is a command line management interface which is becoming more and more widely used for managing the advanced features of Microsoft Server products. AX has a PowerShell management interface and we'll cover that in more detail later in the book, when we discuss deploying code and managing environments. The reports can take a while to deploy; so be patient, nothing has gone wrong!

> **Running Reports on the SSRS Server**
>
> You may find that some components of the Dynamics AX role centers fail to load and generate errors about running the reports on the reporting server, or turning on remote errors. What this is suggesting is that you use the native Reporting Services interface to run the reports in question. If they fail to run, you'll get a far more detailed error message that will save you a lot of time trying to track down the problem.

SQL Analysis Services

Unlike Reporting Services, the initial installation of Analysis Services is fairly straight forward. Having decided which server to install Analysis Services on (in our example the same server cluster as the primary database engine), install Analysis Services, followed by the Dynamics AX Analysis Services role by running Dynamics AX setup.

The post installation tasks for Analysis Services are more complex, and some require work in the AX application after we have configured base settings. When following the installation guide, get as far as installing the Analysis Services role and then come back to the final steps after you have completed the basic application setup.

AX Client and Office Add-ins

The AX client is one of the most straight forward components to install. It is typically installed on each client PC, or on a **Remote Desktop Services** (**RDS**), or on Citrix server; if user access will be by remote application or thin client. When installing on Citrix or RDS servers, be sure to select the Remote Desktop Services integration role as this will allow AX to access your local office applications as well as improving the overall user experience.

A prerequisite warning will be generated if you don't have the Enhanced Desktop Experience Pack installed on the server and don't have the **themes** service running. These components of Windows 2008 server generate a Windows 7 style look and feel (known as Aero), and the AX client has been written to run best with this enabled. AX will run without this interface theme, but will not look or feel as good. Bear this in mind before deploying AX to servers used for client access and work with the infrastructure team to ensure, where possible, that Aero is available and enabled by default for all users.

Remember that you can only install the AX client on a domain joined PC or server, it will not install on a standalone machine. Also, bear in mind that the setup routine will try and contact the AOS server you specify as the default configuration during setup. You need to make sure that you have at least one AOS active before trying to install the client.

The Office Add-in requires Office 2007 or 2010, so make sure one of these is installed first. The prerequisites validator in the Dynamics setup program will make sure you have everything that you need installed, and the setup guide provides detailed step by step instructions.

When asked during setup if you wish to store configuration information in the registry or a file, select **Registry**, as there are some known issues around storing configurations in a file.

Running AX for the first time

As soon as you complete the installation of the object server and database, you can log in to AX. We recommend you to do this using the client on the first AOS server under either the domain administrator account, or a dedicated AX administrator account, which has local admin privileges on the AOS server. The account you first login to AX with will be designated as ADMIN in AX and will have full system administration privileges.

Once the AX client has launched, you will be presented with a post-installation checklist. It is important that you complete all the steps in this checklist to ensure you have a fully functional AX environment.

You will need your license file which should be provided by the partner in order to complete the checklist.

Post checklist tasks

After completing the checklist, there are several other important setup tasks to be completed, which is a good idea to do at this point. As before, this book will not provide detailed information of how to set up these features, but acts as a reminder to ensure that the following are done:

- **Configuring Servers**: If you have installed more than one instance of AX, create a load balance group and add the servers to it. In our example scenario, AOS servers 1 and 2 will be placed in the load balancing group.
- **Designate a batch server**: Mark at least one server as a batch server. In our example, AOS - 3 is to be used for this purpose. Then make sure that the chosen server is assigned to process all your batch groups.

- **Configure reporting servers**: In the reporting server setup, create a configuration for every reporting server AOS combination that is valid. As a minimum, every AOS server a user can connect to must have at least one reporting server configuration marked as default. This is an unusual interface as you will see several records marked as default, but this is correct—without it, you'll find reports won't run on some of your AOS servers.

Installing other environments

Now that we've created LIVE, it's time to create all our other environments from it. This is best done once the installation checklist has been completed in LIVE and following these basic steps:

Copying the LIVE database

Start by shutting down all the LIVE AOS servers. Some information is held in memory on the AOS servers, and is only written to the database once the AOS is shutdown.

Perform a full backup of the LIVE databases, the transactional and baseline DB (and in 2012 R2, the application DB), then restore it using the **Restore File and File Groups** option in SQL Management Studio. This will give you the option to specify a new database name and will ensure the files are created correctly. You can restore the same backup multiple times to create your environments.

Remember to stick to the naming convention, for example, CTO_DAX6_PRELIVE, CTO_DAX6_TEST, and CTO_DAX6_DEV.

The same procedure can be used for copying the LIVE database over the other environments on a periodic basis, for example, when you want to refresh the data in PRE-LIVE.

As we have duplicated the database, we do not need to install the database role for our new environments, and the main function of the database role is to create a blank database.

The new environments will have configuration data from the LIVE environment, which will need to be reconfigured as appropriate.

Installing roles

Now repeat the installation steps outlined previously for each of the new environments, remembering to stick to your naming conventions. In the scenario where you plan to install multiple roles on a single server, for example, TEST and DEV, you may consider using the single server install option then overwriting the database it creates with the backup of LIVE. Note that single server requires all the components to be installed on a single machine. If you plan to leave the database on a central SQL Server, you may want to consider installing the components separately.

Summary

In this chapter, we have discussed what environments to provision and when. We have covered the key components involved in installation to give you an idea of what is involved, and highlighted some potential pitfalls. For detailed instructions, the AX Installation Guide should be consulted at all stages, and the installation team should certainly involve one or more technical experts from the partner.

Once installation of AX environments is complete, we can begin analyzing the requirements and scope of the project. The next chapter will deal with the importance of understanding the business requirements and the Sure Step processes that allow us to do so.

5
Business Requirements Analysis

Understanding the business requirements and ensuring that the detailed requirements have been properly scoped is the focus of the Analysis phase of Sure Step. This is also designed to be the formal project start. The full contractual documentation should be in place as well as project management disciplines. Cross Phase activities should also be firmly established. In the case that these prerequisites are not established, a pause to establish them (or suitable interim measures) is wiser than rushing headlong into an unstructured project, because from this stage, the pressure is unlikely to subside. It is also important to get a grip of budgeting and reporting at this stage.

The key objectives for this phase in Standard, Agile, Rapid, and Upgrade projects include:

- Finalization and approval of the project charter
- Finalization and approval of the project plan
- Execution of the project kick-off meeting
- Documentation and approval of functional requirements
- Execution and documentation of Fit Gap analysis
- Revision of the budget

Additional objectives for the Analysis phase in Enterprise projects include:

- Execution of executive kick-off meetings
- Development of the Organization Change Management strategy, communications strategy, and training strategy
- Documentation and approval of functional and non-functional requirements
- Development of the Future State business process models
- Definition of the master data taxonomy and management process
- Assessment of the architecture and infrastructure

In this chapter, the following topics will be covered:

- Overlap with the Diagnostic phase
- Process or Functional Analysis
- Best practices
- Project team training
- Rebudgeting the program

Overlap with the Diagnostic

Ideally, the Diagnostic phase focusses on identifying business processes and requirements, whereas the Analysis phase focusses on detailing these to a degree that they can be properly designed in the subsequent design phase. The main inputs to the Analysis phase are the documents generated during the Diagnostic phase.

In practice, depending on the project type and how thoroughly requirements were investigated in the diagnostic phase, the state of understanding the project requirements may be ahead of, on target with, or behind the ideal scenario of key requirements being identified.

Assuming that we are in the ideal scenario, the Analysis phase will focus on analysis workshops for each of the business process areas to requirements level. Depending on the project type, analysis may require a simple one pass review of requirements, or in more complex scenarios, iterative evaluation of **Current State (CS)** and **Future State (FS)** processes. The *Business process engineering/reengineering and diagramming* section discusses CS and FS process mapping in more detail, which will be covered later in this chapter.

If more detailed analysis of processes and requirements has already happened during the Diagnostic phase, perhaps during a Proof of Concept or prototype session, it is important to use the kick-off of the Analysis phase as a gateway to review which activities are outstanding from the Diagnostic phase, and which have already been completed from the Analysis phase to ensure that all activities are planned.

Process or functional analysis

Historically, it has been common to understand requirements from more of a functional than a process basis. Evaluating requirements from either of these perspectives should yield the same results; however, experience suggests that this is not always the case. Our experience is that process-based analysis gives better results and improved user experiences during the deployment cycle of a project.

Functional-based identification and analysis of requirements tends to happen where the project is driven from a list of requirements, perhaps originating from tender documentation or feature lists. Process-based identification and analysis tends to put requirements into better context and holistically reviews the impact of requirements across a business. There is a catch here though; usually in process-based analysis, you tend to have a much larger customization list, as you are consistently trying to map system to process and obviously as the business is not using AX, their process will differ from the standard AX flow.

We prefer to start by identifying departments, roles within departments, processes occurring within roles, and finally requirements attached to the roles. This approach lends itself to business process engineering (Current State and Future State), and also to some of the new and emerging features of Dynamics AX such as those listed in the following:

- Role Centers
- The new AX 2012 security paradigm (roles, duties, and permissions privileges)
- Workflow
- Cues and dashboards

Reengineering processes is a significant scope point, which needs to have been agreed during the Diagnostic. Dynamics AX is as capable as being deployed out of the box as it is to be fully customized to extract maximum business value from appropriate process customization. A pragmatic approach to maximizing value, considering future implications, and realizing project timescales and budgets is obviously essential. The most important aspect of project management is agreeing and communicating the scope and then planning to enact what is agreed.

The Sure Step content has become more process centric across recent releases, especially compared to the Navision On Target methodology inherited by Microsoft in the Navision acquisition. Process centered projects are also easier to test and train.

A common belief to avoid is that managers really know the processes followed by their staff. We have found it beneficial to carefully evaluate who is in the analysis sessions and how widely the review and sign off documents should be circulated to ensure proper understanding of requirements and full buy-in from relevant stakeholders.

Another consideration to bear in mind is that some product features of Dynamics AX 2012 are ahead of the methodology content. So, when analyzing and implementing role centers and cues, we may to have to improvise.

Business process engineering/reengineering and diagramming

ERP projects are common vehicles for delivering changed business processes, and we need to start by identifying to what extent they are expected to change. Often business processes are overdue for review, and an ERP project is a convenient time to enact this. Smart customers and partners prefer to fit the business to the system wherever practical rather than vice versa, and approach **Business Process Reengineering** (**BPR**) from this perspective. In this case, it is useful to schedule some introductory training to the DAX product prior to the analysis sessions, or use product demonstrations, or a prototype as part of the analysis workshops.

If processes are expected to change dramatically, it is essential to consider documenting the Current State processes, and then as a separate exercise, documenting the Future State processes. Although this is regarded as tedious by some, it helps to understand the processes thoroughly before reworking them. Occasionally, it is necessary to undertake a second stage of Future State consideration of how the process will be enacted in AX, although this is normally considered a part of the Future State process anyway. Where extensive change is planned, it is important to consider the Sure Step content and guidance related to Organizational Change Management.

If processes are expected to undergo minor revision and update, then an experienced analyst can consider directly undertaking Future State business processes in the first instance. This is also common in vertical and rapid projects, but before making this decision, consider it carefully as more time spent in analysis normally results in less time spent in deployment and testing!

There are many established methods of process engineering, but Sure Step does not dictate any particular method. In particular, major management consultancies tend to have their own methods and tools.

Best practices

The Microsoft Sure Step content includes a wealth of best practice processes charts and role-tailored questionnaires for our consideration. These have been designed around common business processes modelled in the AX product. Check for new Sure Step content (there is a Sure Step parameter tick box to automatically check for updates on startup), as these best practice processes are frequently updated by Microsoft. Updates include reworking the processes to emerging releases of AX and industry specific content.

Despite the availability of this material, it is essential that suitably skilled and experienced analysts are used to identify important and unimportant process variations for clients. This is even more important when working with industry solutions or verticals, which are not a core focus of the standard AX product. Inexperienced consultants working from checklists and process diagrams will soon be rejected by customers.

Master and subprocess list

An important document to create and maintain throughout the project is a list of master and subprocesses. For example, master processes might be vendor creation and a subprocess might be credit checking. Using these lists helps to ensure that training, testing, process guidelines, and security are inclusive of all of the business' key processes. New processes are likely to be uncovered throughout a project, and referring to these checklists is a simple way of ensuring all project requirements are catered for.

Workshops and documentation

Analysis workshops need to be thorough enough to evaluate, if necessary redesign processes, but brief enough not to consume unnecessary time and cost. Many businesses get stuck in very long cycles of process analysis and the results can be of dubious value.

To alleviate this:

- Have an experienced project manager or consultant lead the process
- Carefully evaluate attendees
    - Functionally representative?
    - End users and senior management?
    - Available?
- Understand the full list of processes before starting
- Run a pilot workshop to evaluate the time necessary
- Plan how to document the processes and establish clear templates
- Agree the review and revision process via tracked documentation

Typically, you would undertake:

- Current State workshops producing CS business process diagrams.
- Future State workshops producing FS business process diagrams for processes subject to change.

In addition to the business process documents and functional requirements document, which are the key outputs of this phase, don't forget the:

- Finalization and approval of the project charter
- Finalization and approval of the project plan
- Revision of Fit Gap Analysis and estimates
- Creation of the Work Breakdown Structure and budget
- Detail of the system architecture and requirements
- Outline of the training, testing, and data migration strategies
- Identification of non-standard reporting and workflow requirements

Project team training

Training can be very different from one project to the next due to the type of project being deployed, as well as the capability and structure of the internal and external team.

We like to consider the following when outlining the training plan:

Partner team

Does the partner team need training? New product releases, the use of third party and ISV solutions, and inclusion of less well-used functionality are just some of the factors that should be carefully considered. Experienced AX 2009 consultants can expect a few surprises (most of them pleasant) when implementing AX 2012, including but not limited to:

- Organization hierarchies
- Dimensional framework
- Global address book
- Master data
- Shared tables
- Code models

Customer teams

The customer will generally have several teams which will include an amount of crossover. These may include, but are not limited to:

- Executive
- Steering committee
- Project team
- Key users
- End users

It is important to consider what training is required, and just as importantly when it is required.

We advocate that:

- The project team is trained in the standard product prior to analysis
- At least one team member undertake formal Microsoft curriculum training
    - This material is available free on Customer Source
- Process guidelines are provided to support testing
- The testers are trained in the configured product prior to testing
- Process guidelines are updated prior to end user training
- The end users are trained in the tested product prior to go-live
- Trained users have access to training environment for practice
- All training is subject to pre-course objectives and post-course evaluation

- Post go-live review and training can yield great results
- Peer support can help less familiar users adopt the system

While all of the just listed points seem obvious enough in hindsight, they are common sense more than common practice. It is also necessary in the training plan to agree who will provide the training, as there is a significant cost implication.

Rebudgeting the project

A Fit Gap analysis is commonly enacted during the Diagnostic phase. The Fit Gap analysis identifies all customer requirements, and identifies whether they are a Gap or a Fit. From this Functional Design, documents can be created for Gaps and or Fits. As more details of requirements emerges, it is necessary to revisit the Fit Gap and revise any existing project documentation accordingly.

It is rare for a Fit Gap analysis and estimate not to need revision, but the variance will depend on the skill and diligence with which the diagnostic was enacted. We like to achieve a 75 percent accuracy or a tolerance of plus or minus 25 percent between a Guesstimate and a Diagnostic phase, and a 90 percent accuracy between a Diagnostic and an Analysis phase. Any variance further in the project should be attributable to change requests or unexpected over-run—not incomplete understanding of scope or requirements. The following examples illustrate the Sure Step template provided to analyze the degree of fit, and the number of gaps requiring customization or configuration.

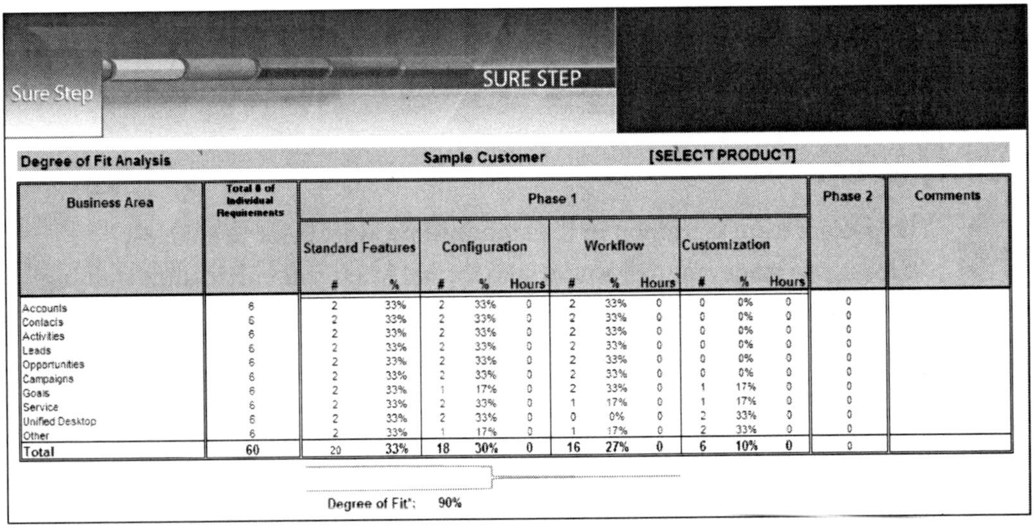
Sure Step
SURE STEP

Degree of Fit Analysis   Sample Customer   [SELECT PRODUCT]

Business Area	Total # of Individual Requirements	Phase 1											Phase 2	Comments
		Standard Features		Configuration			Workflow			Customization				
		#	%	#	%	Hours	#	%	Hours	#	%	Hours		
Accounts	6	2	33%	2	33%	0	2	33%	0	0	0%	0	0	
Contacts	6	2	33%	2	33%	0	2	33%	0	0	0%	0	0	
Activities	6	2	33%	2	33%	0	2	33%	0	0	0%	0	0	
Leads	6	2	33%	2	33%	0	2	33%	0	0	0%	0	0	
Opportunities	6	2	33%	2	33%	0	2	33%	0	0	0%	0	0	
Campaigns	6	2	33%	2	33%	0	2	33%	0	0	0%	0	0	
Goals	6	2	33%	1	17%	0	2	33%	0	1	17%	0	0	
Service	6	2	33%	2	33%	0	1	17%	0	1	17%	0	0	
Unified Desktop	6	2	33%	2	33%	0	0	0%	0	2	33%	0	0	
Other	6	2	33%	1	17%	0	1	17%	0	2	33%	0	0	
Total	60	20	33%	18	30%	0	16	27%	0	6	10%	0	0	

Degree of Fit*: 90%

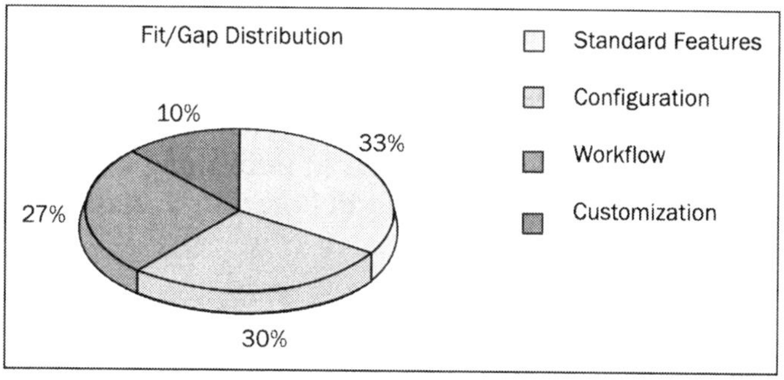

The project plan and budget obviously need revision, and the Project Charter and other key deliverables will need to be revised in line with those changes.

We can expect customer resistance to the revised budgeting and planning—after all, many customers begin a project with a timescale and budget in mind, before they have even decided upon their requirements.

When we prepare a budget for the project, we have found it useful to create a spreadsheet comparing budget, forecast, actual, and variance on a monthly basis using an agreed level of the WBS. See the extracts shown in the next screenshot for an easy template to follow. This is not a Sure Step template, but is available from the author on request. It is of course useful to ensure that timesheets, invoices, and the project plans are detailed to the same level of the WBS. The example following uses the simple expedient of analysis time by individual. Although this is easy to reconcile, it doesn't give a lot of detail on progress—although, that is of course the function of the project plan.

Budget structure

We have developed the budget template as shown in the following screenshot for giving control where there is not an appropriate system in place. This template is only a suggestion and is available from the Packt Publishing website free of charge. The spreadsheet has tabs for **Budget**, **Invoiced**, **Forecast**, **Variance**, and **Summary**; each of which are reviewed as follows:

BUDGET

	WBS	September	October	November	December	January	February	March	April	May	June	Budget	Unallocated	TOTAL
Total Cost		122,232	142,582	92,582	41,990	74,010	234,610	49,010	73,810	43,960	44,350	961,470	42,334	1,003,804
Total Capital Cost		115,832	142,582	92,582	41,990	69,010	206,010	46,010	68,810	38,960	39,350	907,070	45,934	953,004
Capital Non Licence Costs		75,832	142,582	92,582	41,990	56,510	46,010	46,010	68,810	38,960	39,350	692,070	43,434	735,504
PB	2.1	5,000	5,000	5,000	5,000	5,000	4,500	4,500	4,500	4,500	6,000	40,000	-9,000	31,000
AH	2.2	4,500	4,500	4,500	4,500	4,500	4,500	4,500	4,500	4,500	4,500	30,000	-15,000	15,000
EH	2.3	2,000	2,000	2,000	2,000	2,000	2,000	2,000	2,000	2,000	2,000		-20,000	-20,000
MB	2.4	6,750	6,750	6,750	6,750	6,750	6,750	6,750	6,750	6,750	6,750	67,500	0	67,500
AJ	2.5	2,632	2,632	2,632	1,880	3,760	3,760	3,760	3,760	0	0	26,320	1,504	27,824
AT	2.6	4,200	4,200	4,200	4,200	4,200	4,200	4,200	4,200	4,200	4,200	42,000	0	42,000
AB	2.7	6,000	6,000	6,000	6,160	8,800	8,800	8,800	6,600	5,500	4,400	88,000	20,940	108,940
Hardware	3.1	25,000	100,000	50,000		10,000			25,000	10		210,000	-10	209,990
External Training Courses	4	8,250										8,250	0	8,250
Expenses	9	11,500	11,500	11,500	11,500	11,500	11,500	11,500	11,500	11,500	11,500	180,000	65,000	245,000
														0
Capital Licence Costs		40,000	0	0	0	12,500	160,000	0	0	0	0	215,000	2,500	217,500
Dynamics AX Licence	5.1	40,000					160,000					200,000	0	200,000
BI 4 Dynamics Licence	5.2					12,500						15,000	2,500	17,500
														0
Recurring Costs		6,400	0	0	0	5,000	28,600	3,000	5,000	5,000	5,000	54,400	-3,600	50,800
Recurring Licence Costs		6,400	0	0	0	2,000	25,600	0	0	0	0	34,400	400	34,800
Dynamics AX Licence	6.1	6,400	0	0	0	0	25,600	0	0	0	0	32,000	0	32,000
BI 4 Dynamics Licence	6.2	0	0	0	0	2,000	0	0	0	0	0	2,400	400	2,800
														0
Recurring Non Licence Costs		0	0	0	0	3,000	3,000	3,000	5,000	5,000	5,000	20,000	-4,000	16,000
Vendor support contract	7	0	0	0	0	3,000	3,000	3,000	5,000	5,000	5,000	20,000	-4,000	16,000

Firstly, we enter the budget into the **Budget** tab. The budget should be split into measurable chunks, and we must be careful to only consider using a Work Breakdown Structure (WBS) level which is feasible to measure—refer to the *Work Breakdown Structure* section in *Chapter 1, Installing and Setting up sure Step* for more on the WBS. We will also want to compare these costs with project progress, normally via a project plan (see *Chapter 11, Deployment Phase* for more details).

Having entered the budget at a periodic (usually monthly) basis, the unallocated column is for agreed budget that is not allocated to specific periods and/or for contingency. The unallocated column has conditional formatting to show whether the imbalance between the budget and total is good or bad.

INVOICED

	WBS	September	October	November	December	January	February	March	April	May	June	TOTAL
Total Cost		135,938	159,088	0	0	0	0	0	0	0	0	295,026
												0
Total Capital Cost		129,538	159,088	0	0	0	0	0	0	0	0	288,626
												0
Capital Non Licence Costs		89,538	159,088	0	0	0	0	0	0	0	0	248,626
PB	2.1	10,528	10,528									21,056
AH	2.2	8,100	8,100									16,200
EH	2.3	2,000	2,000									4,000
MB	2.4	10,528	10,528									21,056
AJ	2.5	2,632	2,632									5,264
AT	2.6	4,200	10,000									14,200
KD	2.7	8,800	8,800									17,600
Hardware	3.1	23,000	95,000									118,000
External Training Courses	4	8,250										8,250
Expenses	9	11,500	11,500									23,000
												0
Capital Licence Costs		40,000	0									40,000
Dynamics AX Licence	5.1	40,000										40,000
BI 4 Dynamics Licence	5.2											0
												0
Recurring Costs		6,400	0									6,400
												0
Recurring Licence Costs		6,400	0	0	0	0	0	0	0	0	0	6,400
Dynamics AX Licence	6.1	6,400	0	0	0	0	0	0	0	0	0	6,400
BI 4 Dynamics Licence	6.2	0	0	0	0	0	0	0	0	0	0	0
												0
Recurring Non Licence Costs		0										0
Vendor support contract	7	0										0

The **Invoiced** tab simply allows us to enter the actual invoice summary, which is generally done on a monthly basis.

FORECAST

INVOICED BUDGET

	WBS	September	October	November	December	January	February	March	April	May	June	TOTAL
Total Cost		*135,938*	*159,088*	*92,582*	*41,990*	*74,010*	*234,610*	*49,010*	*73,810*	*43,960*	*44,350*	*949,348*
Total Capital Cost		***129,538***	***159,088***	***92,582***	***41,990***	***69,010***	***206,010***	***46,010***	***68,810***	***38,960***	***39,350***	***891,348***
Capital Non Licence Costs		*89,538*	*159,088*	*92,582*	*41,990*	*56,510*	*46,010*	*46,010*	*68,810*	*38,960*	*39,350*	*678,848*
PB	2.1	10,528	10,528	5,000	5,000	5,000	4,500	4,500	4,500	4,500	6,000	60,056
AH	2.2	8,100	8,100	4,500	4,500	4,500	4,500	4,500	4,500	4,500	4,500	52,200
EH	2.3	2,000	2,000	2,000	2,000	2,000	2,000	2,000	2,000	2,000	2,000	20,000
MB	2.4	10,528	10,528	6,750	6,750	6,750	6,750	6,750	6,750	6,750	6,750	75,056
AJ	2.5	2,632	2,632	2,632	1,880	3,760	3,760	3,760	3,760	0	0	24,816
AT	2.6	4,200	10,000	4,200	4,200	4,200	4,200	4,200	4,200	4,200	4,200	47,800
KD	2.7	8,800	8,800	6,000	6,160	8,800	8,800	8,800	6,600	5,500	4,400	72,660
Hardware	3.1	23,000	95,000	50,000	0	10,000	0	0	25,000	10	0	203,010
External Training Courses	4	8,250	0	0	0	0	0	0	0	0	0	8,250
Expenses	9	11,500	11,500	11,500	11,500	11,500	11,500	11,500	11,500	11,500	11,500	115,000
		0	0	0	0	0	0	0	0	0	0	0
Capital Licence Costs		*40,000*	*0*	*0*	*0*	*12,500*	*160,000*	*0*	*0*	*0*	*0*	*212,500*
Dynamics AX Licence	5.1	*40,000*	0	0	0	0	160,000	0	0	0	0	200,000
BI 4 Dynamics Licence	5.2	*0*	0	0	0	12,500	0	0	0	0	0	12,500
Recurring Costs		***6,400***	***0***	***0***	***0***	***5,000***	***28,600***	***3,000***	***5,000***	***5,000***	***5,000***	***58,000***
Recurring Licence Costs		*6,400*	*0*	*0*	*0*	*2,000*	*25,600*	*0*	*0*	*0*	*0*	*34,000*
Dynamics AX Licence	6.1	*6,400*	0	0	0	0	25,600	0	0	0	0	32,000
BI 4 Dynamics Licence	6.2	*0*	0	0	0	2,000	0	0	0	0	0	2,000
Recurring Non Licence Costs		*0*	*0*	*0*	*0*	*3,000*	*3,000*	*3,000*	*5,000*	*5,000*	*5,000*	*24,000*
Vendor support contract	7	*0*	0	0	0	3,000	3,000	3,000	5,000	5,000	5,000	24,000

Secondly, the forecast is entered. Initially this would match the budget (less the unallocated amounts). As the invoiced amounts are entered into the **Invoiced** tab each month, the same column should be copied to the **Forecast** tab. Over time, the forecast figures are a combination of actual to date and budget for the future.

We want to keep the initial budget for evaluation; so the forecast allows us to compare actual invoicing (up to date) and our budget (going forward), so that we can see the **Cost to Complete** (CTC) and the difference between CTC and the original budget.

VARIANCE

	WBS	September	October	November	December	January	February	March	April	May	June	TOTAL
Total Cost		13,706	16,506									30,212
		0	0									
Total Capital Cost		**13,706**	**16,506**									**30,212**
		0	**0**									
Capital Non Licence Costs		13,706	16,506									30,212
PB	2.1	5,528	5,528									11,056
AH	2.2	3,600	3,600									7,200
EH	2.3	0	0									0
MB	2.4	3,778	3,778									7,556
AJ	2.5	0	0									0
AT	2.6	0	5,800									5,800
KD	2.7	2,800	2,800									5,600
Hardware	3.1	-2,000	-5,000									-7,000
External Training Courses	4	0	0									0
Expenses	9	0	0									0
		0	0									
Capital Licence Costs		*0*	*0*									*0*
Dynamics AX Licence	5.1	*0*	*0*									*0*
BI 4 Dynamics Licence	5.2	*0*	*0*									*0*
		0	0									0
Recurring Costs		***0***	***0***									***0***
Recurring Licence Costs		*0*	*0*									*0*
Dynamics AX Licence	6.1	*0*	*0*									*0*
BI 4 Dynamics Licence	6.2	*0*	*0*									*0*
		0	0									
Recurring Non Licence Costs		*0*	*0*									*0*
Vendor support contract	7	*0*	*0*									*0*

Having entered the invoicing figure, the **Variance** tab shows where the actuals vary from the budget, with appropriate colour coding to analyze the significant variance.

V 0.01 **Updated** 01/07/2012 **Editor** Keith Dunkinson

Microsoft Dynamics ERP System Project Financials

	September	October	November	December	January	February	March	April	May	June	Budget	Unallocated	TOTAL
Budget	122,232	142,582	92,582	41,990	74,010	234,610	49,010	73,810	43,960	44,350		42,334	961,470
Invoiced	135,938	159,088	0	0	0	0	0	0	0	0			295,026
Variance	13,706	16,506	0	0	0	0	0	0	0	0			30,212
Forecast	135,938	159,088	92,582	41,990	74,010	234,610	49,010	73,810	43,960	44,350	949,348		949,348

We also have concise project costs summary generated from the data we have entered.

This spreadsheet is the one we use and modify frequently. It should provide a basis or ideas for generating your own. It would of course be easy to add much more depth and complexity, but be mindful that what you make you need to maintain!

Sample project

Although our sample project was an Agile Sure Step project, we were able to identify the processes and produce a high-level Functional Requirements Document (FRD) at the outset. Because the processes and departments were subject to a high level of change and since we had short timescales, we went straight to the Future State processes. These were reviewed, prototyped, and demonstrated to stakeholders repeatedly throughout the project as the system was developed.

To support the coordination of the project, we developed an agile management tool, which identified all processes, reports, migrations, integrations, developments, and so on at a subprocess level. This enabled easy reporting of progress by process and individual. There are many commercially available tools, one example is Eylean Tasks. None of the tools I have seen are useful without consideration and setup to meet your own preferences.

Summary

The Analysis phase (or collection of business requirements) needs to be carefully planned, or it will take much longer than expected. Sure Step provides a wealth of content and guidance, which we have previously discussed in this chapter. The amount of change that is expected to occur is the most important thing to consider when planning the analysis, and at the end of the process, a review of budgeting and planning is necessary. AX 2012 includes many new and changed features, and familiarity with the products being deployed is a prerequisite to good Future State analysis.

In this chapter, we have learnt about the overlap between the Diagnostic and Analysis phases, and the importance of being thorough and detailed in these stages, while maintaining a dynamic approach to the ever-changing structure of a project. We have discussed important objectives of this phase including the Fit Gap analysis, revision of the budget, and finalization of project initiation documents.

In the next chapter, we will be looking at the more technical side of the AX setup and configuration, and focus on some important factors that will help to get the implementation heading in the right direction from the beginning of the project.

6
AX Setup

In the previous chapter, we discussed the final analysis and scoping exercise which should have resulted in a clear set of business requirements. During the analysis workshops, Dynamics AX should have been used to illustrate concepts, demonstrate standard functionality, and prototype potential configurations. It is possible that some base configuration will have already been done during the workshops, which is fine as long as the configuration was done with the live environment in mind and not as a "quick fix" to enable some functionality for demo or test.

In this chapter, we will discuss the basic setup required to make AX usable and in particular, the decisions which need to be made. As this book is not a technical "how-to" for installing and configuring AX, we will not provide instructions on how to configure the system itself. This is a job for the Partner. Rather, we will discuss the key decisions that need to be made and whose importance is often overlooked. We will try, where possible, to provide practical examples from our own experience to help guide your thinking and help you avoid some of the most common mistakes.

This chapter will cover the following topics:

- System-wide configuration
- Financial dimensions
- Module configuration

System-wide configuration

The functionality in Dynamics AX is organized into modules. Each module has its own setup section that contains parameters and options that control the functionality in that module. There are some features that span multiple modules or have no place in a specific module, these we consider to be system-wide and often find that they have to be set up in order for other parts of the system to function.

In this section, we will discuss some of the system-wide configurations and the points to consider when deciding how to configure them.

Configuration keys

The functionality of Dynamics AX is not only sorted into modules but into features within those modules. Features can be turned on or off through the use of **configuration keys**. One of the first tasks after installing AX is to review the list of configuration keys and enable or disable the features you'll need. This activity is almost always done by the partner and usually doesn't require much input from the customer provided a comprehensive requirements analysis has been done. Note that configuration keys are application wide and therefore apply to all companies. This means that country-specific features required only in some companies will in fact be available in all.

Some of the most common features controlled by configuration keys are country-specific features, for example, Italian VAT rules. If your company does not, and has no immediate plan to operate in Italy, there would be no need to enable this feature. However, if you do operate in Italy but don't plan to roll out AX there just yet, but may do so in future, it would be wise to enable the configuration key but not configure the functionality. The reason for this is that enabling and disabling configuration keys can affect how the system operates. If you know you might need the functionality in future, it is best to enable it during the early stages of the project before you go live. This means all your testing is performed with the functionality enabled but not configured. If and when you come to use it, all you have to do is configure the features and test the results. There should be no regression in application functionality because the configuration key was always enabled.

There is one exception to this, the Telephony Integration configuration key. This enables a TAPI interface between AX and a TAPI-enabled phone system. TAPI is now quite old and is becoming less and less popular as an interface mechanism between business and telephony systems. AX 2012 introduced tight integration between Lync (Microsoft's Unified Communications Platform) and AX which, if practical, should be used in preference to TAPI. In our own experience, the TAPI interface has been known to cause some problems and instabilities in the AX client when used in combination with other telephony-enabled software. For this reason, only enable TAPI support if you are sure you are going to use it. Unlike some other configuration keys, enabling it later is relatively risk free and thus it is better left switched off until needed, however Microsoft has announced that the TAPI features will be deprecated in the next version of AX.

Number sequences

In Dynamics AX, **number sequence** is the term used to describe the unique references that are assigned to new records created in the AX database. All number sequences in AX have been abstracted into a setup framework that allows us to centrally configure and manage the references used in our system. AX 2012 has added new functionality to the number sequence system, namely the ability to share a number sequence across multiple companies.

There is a built-in wizard that will create a number sequence for every record type that needs one, however, the number sequences it creates are not usually in line with the sequences a company would choose hence almost everyone decides to change them.

Based on our own practical experience, the following points should be considered when designing number sequences:

- **Volume of records**: If you create 1,000 orders per day, a sales order number sequence with five digits will only last for 99 days of trading. Conversely, if you currently have 3,000 customers and your growth is likely to be consistent, why implement a number sequence for customer account longer than four digits. Note that it is relatively easy to increase the length of number sequences later but decreasing them will obviously present issues.
- **Numeric or alpha-numeric**: Many are tempted to include letters in the number sequence as either a prefix or suffix. This can help to quickly identify what a reference refers to when seen out of context, for example, if we use a four-digit number for both customers and suppliers, 5023, could refer to a customer or supplier. Prefixing customers with a "C" and suppliers with an "S" would make it immediately recognizable. However, it's worth bearing the following in mind when choosing to add alpha characters:
    - **Speed of entry**: How often will the reference be typed? It's quicker for users to stay on the numeric keypad than to have to enter a mix of letters and numbers.
    - **Available hardware**: Does the reference need to be entered into any third-party system and do they have any limitations? Industrial systems often don't have full keyboards so make sure you don't incorporate characters that are not easily available or require a function key to access.
    - **Numeric entry**: Using an interactive telephone system for example. If you use numeric customer account codes, it's very simple to enter it with a touch-tone phone. Alpha characters would add complexity to the software and the instructions to the users, and would increase the risk of data entry error and user frustration.

    - **Barcoding**: Consider if the reference needs to be represented as a barcode anywhere and check that the symbology supports the characters you choose.
    - Based on the previous example, similar results can be achieved without alpha characters by choosing to start customer accounts at 1000 and supplier accounts at 5000.
- **Avoid confusable characters**: This refers to letters and numbers that can be confused with each other, for example: zero "0" and the letter "O"; one "1" and the letter "I". The most common example of this is the prefix people choose for the sale order number sequence - SO001234.
- **Be careful**: When creating structured codes or references where each segment means something for example, let's take the product code 01081234; where 01 is the item group, 08 is the subgroup, and 1234 is the item number. While this might seem like a good idea, and there are situations in which this is the best approach, you need to consider why you are doing it. There are several limitations and problems to be aware of before deciding on structured codes:
    - By default, number sequences in AX are simple incrementing numbers and modification or manual entry is required to achieve the kind of coding structure outlined here.
    - Consider the use of separator characters in the same way we considered alpha characters (shown previously).
    - The item lookup in AX is searchable by more than just the item code. You can also place an alias against an item, which you can enter instead of the code.
    - Think about reporting and analysis. AX will be unaware of the meaning assigned to your segments and extra code will have to be written to separate out the values so that they can be used in reports and cubes. AX is designed around separating meaningful data into distinct fields. Consider whether you would be better adding extra fields to AX rather than incorporating the data into a code.
- **Be consistent**: Where possible, try to stick to a convention, for example, if you choose to use a three-character alpha prefix for a number sequence, try and make all your alpha prefixes three characters long. Consistency helps user adoption and reduces data entry errors.
- **Setting starting values**: When continuing a number sequence used in a previous system, or when using starting points to differentiate between different types (see previous example), make sure you set the start values correctly before you start entering transactions as it can be difficult to change later.

Setting up all the number sequences required by AX in one go is a long and arduous task that not many complete. Instead of trying to complete all the setup in one go, define a clear policy for creating number sequences, detailing the format, and conventions that should be adhered to.

> **Create a number sequence master**
>
> Consider nominating someone to be responsible for number sequence configuration. Requests to set up new sequences should go through this person who will ensure that number sequence setup conforms to the policy you established.

Address setup

As an international product, Dynamics AX has specific features to deal with address formatting in different countries. Based on the country you select, AX will ask users to complete different fields and allow selections from drop-down lists with data specifically for that country. AX also has features that allow you to decide how the address should be arranged when printed on documents like sales invoices or purchase orders, to take into account the different address standards in different countries. If you trade with, or have operations in more than one country, this is an important step.

A wizard, which is automatically run as part of the initial setup, creates address formats for some of the more common countries, like the USA and UK with a lookup requirement on ZIP/postcodes however no lookup data for ZIP or postal codes is populated. One of the most common changes people make to this configuration is to turn off the lookup on the ZIP/postcode and the state/county fields and allow free text entries. This is often done so that users can start entering test data to get the system up and running and often ends up being left this way after moving it into live operation. A few years later, people regret this decision when they can't perform sensible analysis by, say, county because they have "N. Yorks", "N Yorks", "North Yorks", "N. Yorkshire", "NorthYorkshire", and so on; all meaning North Yorkshire.

The best way to get started with clean and valid data is to leave the restrictions in place, and in some cases tighten them, and set out to populate the underlying reference tables for ZIP/postcodes, state/county, and so on. If you plan to import customers and suppliers with address details, the import routine should be written to "find or insert" values in the lookup tables, meaning that your base data is built as a result of your import. Of course, if you choose to use this method, you'll need to cleanse the data before importing, to remove the duplication issues previously highlighted.

Data cleansing and address formatting are two areas where everyone sets out with good intentions but the work is often scaled back due to time constraints. Proper planning and starting on these tasks early is the best way to ensure that you import clean and usable data into AX without carrying forward the dirty data of your previous system.

Document management

Dynamics AX includes document management functionality that allows file attachments or notes to be associated with almost any record in AX database. Buttons included on forms allow users to access the document management form to create, view, or edit the files and notes found. Used correctly, document management in AX can be a very powerful tool for improving the organization, security, and accessibility of files which nearly always deliver productivity gains. For example, using document handling to store electronic copies of purchase invoices against the supplier transaction provides much faster and wider access than a paper original which is useful both in day-to-day operations and during audits. The document management functionality is configured in the Organization module and is fairly straightforward. Following are some tips for key configuration decisions:

- **Storage location**: AX offers the choice of storing files attached through document management in the AX database or in a file share. While the database might seem like the most obvious choice, it is important to consider the volume and size of the files you will attach and to make sure you have enough storage space on the high performance data volume used by your SQL server. It will also have a direct impact on the size of your AX database and thus needs to be considered when creating copies of the *live* database for non-live environments. If you plan to make heavy use of document handling, you may find that using the filesystem is a more practical and cost efficient choice. Seek guidance and input from IT when making this decision.
- **File types**: Only file extensions that have been explicitly configured as allowed can be uploaded to AX document management. The most common file types, for example `.doc`, `.docx`, `.xls`, `.xlsx`, `.pdf`, and so on, are preconfigured but if you plan to upload files generated by specialist applications, you may need to add their file extensions to the list.

- **Document types**: Document types are identifiers that can be defined to further refine the categorization of the notes and files uploaded to AX. AX comes preconfigured with some document types such as Note and File but if you plan to make serious use of document management, we would suggest replacing these with more descriptive entries, for example, a scanned purchase invoice document type might be, Document Type ID: **PL-INV** and Description: **Purchase Invoice**. The document type also defines the type of attachment - an uploaded file or a note entered directly into AX. They can also be used to override the default storage path allowing you to direct the attachments for specific document types to specific places.

A new option available in the document type's form in AX 2012 is the ability to select "Document Library" as the attachment option, in addition to file, note, and so on. The Document Library option is designed to be used in conjunction with a SharePoint library and the new Office Connectors. By creating Word Templates built from queries defined in Dynamic AX, it is possible to create "Mail Merge" style documents that can be populated with data directly from AX. By uploading these templates into a SharePoint library and then entering the path to that library against an AX Document Type set as Document Library, the Word Templates become available in AX. Based on the queries used in the templates, AX automatically deduces the data context required to merge the document and only makes it available when document handling is called for a compatible record. For example, a "New Customer Welcome Letter" that uses the Customer table as its primary data source would only be available when document handling was launched for a customer record. When creating a new document using this method, AX automatically merges the data with the template, creates a new document, saves it, attaches it into document management, and then opens it for editing. This is a very powerful new feature introduced in AX 2012 and there are some good tutorials and "how-to's" available online that explain these features more fully.

Companies and organizations

Dynamics AX has always had the ability to hold multiple companies within a single database. The process of creating and copying companies was very simple and it was common practice to create a separate company for each legal entity whose accounts would be produced by AX, and then create copies of them for testing purposes. In AX 2012, the functionality around companies and organizations has been enhanced significantly and the approach used with previous versions is no longer valid. This is especially true for "test" companies, which now need to be in their own environment; the duplicate company feature has been removed from this release. Exporting a company and reimporting it back into the same environment can lead to referential integrity problems due to the way the foreign keys are now generated (and the way the data is shared across companies).

The configuration of companies and organizations is now significantly more detailed, but has created far tighter integration between the financial analysis features of the general ledger and business processes organizational structure setup.

Because of the intrinsic links to financial analysis, the setup of organizational structure is normally assigned to those responsible for finance. In previous versions of AX this made sense, as an AX company typically represented a legal entity. Financial dimensions were used to provide more granular department and cost-centric analysis and again, they were typically configured by finance.

In AX 2012, we would still expect to have significant involvement from finance but should also consider involving other departments as the organization structure now has implications for:

- **Security**: The organizational structure is used when setting up security roles and managing access, for example, a user can transact across different organizational structures, based on the process they are executing, rather than the company context they are in.
- **Hierarchies**: The organizational modeling features in AX 2012 allow legal entities and operating units to be organized hierarchically to reflect the actual structure of your organization. This hierarchy can be used to control approval, access, and escalation rights in workflow which is more relevant to business process than finance.
- **Data sharing**: Many of the tables connected with organizational structure are automatically shared across all legal entities (companies) and operating units. This makes sharing system-wide data simpler but needs to be considered up front to ensure that other down-stream modules have access to the relevant shared data.

The tools provided for organizational modeling in AX 2012 are considerably more powerful than the previous versions and even allow graphical modeling of the organizational structure. By including the organizational units as financial dimensions, reporting can be built based on the hierarchy, and "before and after" features even allow reporting based on new "proposed" structures as well as those currently active to compare differences.

Before making any firm decisions and committing the configuration to the *live* system, make sure you create a shared understanding of:

- **The actual structure of the company**: Both from a legal entity perspective and operational perspective.

- **The requirements for reporting and analysis**: Unlike previous versions, it is possible to create a distinct **Profit and Loss** (**P&L**) at business-unit level, and not just at the legal-entity level.
- **The capabilities of Dynamics AX**: What organizational units represent and what they can control. Consider how they will affect reporting, security, and data access.

Financial dimensions

In Dynamics AX, financial dimensions are analysis fields that can be associated with base data, such as customers, items, and so on. This is then copied and merged on transitional records, such as sales orders; and finally posted as part of financial transactions to the general ledger. Transactions within G/L accounts can then be broken down by dimension.

When used correctly they are an incredibly powerful feature that improves data entry, provides extremely flexible and detailed reporting, and significantly reduces the size and complexity of the chart of accounts structure.

Financial dimensions in action – a practical example

We will now focus on financial dimensions and how they can assist with analysis more effectively than using a traditional ledger structure. Let's take mobile phone costs; where we want to be able to analyze these costs by department and employee.

Using a traditional ledger structure

In a traditional ledger system, we would see the following structure in the chart of accounts. The structure XXX-XX-XX refers to account-department-employee.

Account code	Account	Department	Employee
500-00-00	Mobile phones		
500-01-00	Mobile phones	Sales department	
500-01-20	Mobile phones	Sales department	Bob Smith
500-01-47	Mobile phones	Sales department	Jane Doe
500-02-00	Mobile phones	Operations department	
500-02-16	Mobile phones	Operations department	Frank Wright
500-02-82	Mobile phones	Operations department	Emma Jones

In this example, we see that a separate ledger account was created for each employee within each department. Header accounts are also created to illustrate the structure although they will not be posted to and so are not strictly necessary. This method has the following limitations and problems:

- The chart of accounts has to be manually maintained to enforce the same coding structure and codes across all accounts
- Accounts become obsolete but still exist within the chart, for example if Emma Jones moved from Ops to Sales she would need a new account 500-01-82 and her old one would no longer be valid
- Posting transactions in journals or the purchase ledger involves knowing or looking up hundreds or even thousands of codes
- Specialist reporting functions are required to allow reporting and consolidation by code segment, for example to get a list of all sales department costs, a trial balance would have to be run for "???-01-??"

Using financial dimensions

Now let's look at the same requirement using financial dimensions. We have one general ledger account:

- **500**: Mobile phones

We have two financial dimensions linked, in this case, to other data tables in AX:

- **Department**: Linked to Business Units in the organization hierarchy
- **Employee**: Linked to the Employee List in the HR module

We can then enforce, through accounting structure setup and rules, that postings to G/L account 500 must also contain a valid value for the financial dimensions - Department and Employee. The net effect is posting to an account code that looks like this:

- 500-SALES-EMP20
- 500-OPS-EMP82

The key difference is that the account code is dynamic and *not* a real G/L account. The dimensional data is held against the transactions and can be used to segment the data for reporting. This provides the following advantages over the traditional ledger system:

- It allows the chart of accounts to be much shorter and reduces the number of redundant accounts that will accumulate over time.

- It allows very detailed analysis of balances within G/L accounts, limited only by the number of dimensions you create. Because it doesn't require accounts to be created manually, more data is likely to be held at a detailed level, for example all employee costs could be broken down by the Employee dimension. This is not typically done in traditional ledgers as it requires too much effort to set up, maintain, and post to.
- It removes the need for manual maintenance of structures in the G/L and all the dimensional values are either looked up from elsewhere in AX or held in separate tables.
- It allows easy restructuring of ledger accounts for future transactions without creating dead codes, for example Emma Jones would have her department changed on her employee record and would then appear under sales.
- It allows multiple views (financial statements) to be built of a single chart of accounts more easily and with less consideration than with the traditional system, for example by department, cost center, or employee.

Deciding on dimensions

In previous versions of AX, this was quite easy. The standard license came with three financial dimensions called Department, Cost Centre, and Purpose; that you could rename and use as you wished. Additional dimensions could be added but each additional dimension carried a license fee and so most implementations worked within the confines of three dimensions or purchased one or two extra.

In AX 2012, the whole dimension framework has been completely rewritten and now allows the addition of more dimensions without additional cost. Further, dimension values can now be based on lookups from other AX tables, as shown in our previous example, where we based our Employee dimension on the employee code from the HR module. While overall these are positive changes, caution should be exercised when deciding which custom dimensions to add, as the practicalities of working with them outside of journals and purchase ledger screens is significantly different to previous versions of AX, and could have a big impact on the level of development customization required by your system.

These are the key points to consider when adding custom dimensions based on our practical experience of implementing Dynamics AX 2012.

What analysis is really required at General Ledger level

A dimension's primary function is to facilitate analysis at G/L level. Although it is tempting to try and analyze everything at the G/L (and this is certainly the request of many finance people) ask yourself "Do I really need to?". For example, you might include some additional attributes from the item record as dimensions on a sales order, so that you can analyze sales income by these attributes. The question is, why does that analysis need to be done in the G/L and not in the Sales module where there is additional information such as quantity and weight available? It may be a good idea to pass item group through as a dimension to allow you to have one G/L account for Sales Income that you can then segment by your major product categories, but any further analysis is typically (not always) best left in the source module.

A good test is to think about the questions the analysis will raise. For instance, separating total sales revenue out into major product categories at the G/L seems sensible and something that finance will be required to do. Will they be required to separate that same total by individual customer? If so, would extra information be required such as the products they bought, in what quantities, and at what margin? This information is available from the Sales module which has been specifically designed to hold this data in a reportable format. Try not to encourage analysis in the G/L via dimensions when it is best done elsewhere.

Adding dimensions that reference other tables

This refers to adding dimensions that get their values from other AX tables, something that wasn't possible without development before AX 2012. This is a very useful feature as it allows us to include dimensions with validated values, built completely automatically from our existing data.

Let's take our example of an Employee dimension. Before AX 2012, we would have re-used one of our three dimensions (normally, Purpose as it was the lowest level and most granular) and created a values list with all our employees in it. We would also have maintained that list in the HR module with no enforced validation between the two. Every time a new employee was hired, both the HR module and the dimension list would need to be updated.

In AX 2012, we can create a new dimension linked directly to the HR module. Every time a new employee is hired, they are added to the HR module and thus available in the Employee dimension list.

This is a great example of this new 2012 feature in action. Another good example would be to add a dimension linked to the fixed asset list to allow costs, such as repairs to assets, to be posted against the asset code without being posted through the fixed asset module. This would facilitate detailed analysis of costs by fixed asset which was not possible in previous versions without maintaining a separate dimension and values list manually.

But don't be tempted to go too far. You could post the customer or supplier account number, the item code, or project number as a custom dimension, facilitating a great deal of analysis at G/L level that you've never had before. But ask yourself "Do I need it?".

What does analyzing sales revenue by customer at the G/L really give you that the customer sales reports don't? If we didn't have dimensions we would never consider posting that level of detail to the G/L, creating one or more lines for every customer. Just because we can do it relatively easily with a dimension, doesn't mean we should.

Setting dimensions programmatically

Something that comes as a great surprise to first time AX 2012 users, after they have added all their custom dimensions based on lookups to other tables, is the fact that AX doesn't automatically populate obvious dimensions. Let's say we did add the customer account number as a custom dimension (I'm not suggesting that you should), it now appears everywhere that financial dimensions are used. This includes the customer record itself. Many people are shocked to discover that AX hasn't worked out the relationship between the dimension and the customer record, and automatically populated the customer account dimension with the customer account number. They are even more surprised when they are given a development estimate for making the value default automatically.

Think very carefully about how you expect to use these dimensions and how you expect them to be populated in day-to-day operation. The employee and the fixed asset number are both good examples as they will typically be filled in by a user during invoice posting or in a journal. A customer account number or project ID however, would need auto-populating when records are created in those tables in order for the standard dimension copy and merge code to work.

Dimension validation

Validation of dimension combinations was available in previous versions, but was not as widely used; possibly due to the perceived complexity in setup. This has been much improved in AX 2012, but still represents a significant investment in time to configure correctly.

Dimension validation allows rules to be created to enforce certain dimensional values based on the G/L account we are posting to. In our earlier example, we said that the Mobile phone account (500) would require two dimensions, Department and Employee.

Dimension validation can go further and enforce specific combinations, for example, not allowing you to select a department of Ops and an employee from Sales. This is extremely useful when devolving responsibility for coding transactions to the more operational users, as the system is able to enforce valid posting combinations, considerably reducing the number of incorrect posts.

AX 2012 actually goes one step further and allows you, through setup, to dictate different coding structures in different circumstances, for example:

- G/L Account - Department - Employee
- Department - Employee - G/L Account

Using the validation setup, AX is able to filter the list of available results based on the previously selected values. For example, if Sales was selected as the department, then only employees assigned to Sales would be shown. Further, after selecting a department and employee in our second structure shown previously, we would only see a list of G/L accounts that accept this type of posting.

When considering dimensions, make sure finance teams in particular fully understand the capabilities of the dimension framework and how to configure its features, including validation and structures. Make sure sufficient time and resources are allocated to allow a new G/L and dimensional structure to be designed, implemented, and tested. Extra time spent upfront will pay dividends in terms of analysis, reporting, and ease of data entry once AX is in live use.

Module configuration

There are thousands of parameters and setup options across the AX modules. The setup and configuration of these parameters is typically handled by the partner, either based on the analysis and solution design or in collaborative workshops with the customer. Exactly which parameters are to be used and how they will be set up is unique to almost every installation, as their configuration can dramatically affect AX's functionality which, as we know, is tailored to each client's requirements.

A great deal of customization can be achieved through correct configuration of standard functionality; in many cases a modification to the application can be avoided through correct configuration of standard functionality. A real life example of this comes from a company who, after using AX for several years, requested a modification that would automatically update the delivery dates on Sales Order lines when the dates were changed on the Sales Order header. They were about to sign off the development budget when they discovered it was a standard feature of AX and just needed configuring in **Sales Ledger** | **Setup** | **Parameters** | **Sales Order Updates**.

This example highlights the importance of working with a team that fully understands the standard AX system, and with particular expertise and experience in the modules you will use. Correct use of standard functionality delivers the following benefits:

- Delivers the functionality you need in the shortest amount of time through configuration rather than development
- Helps you maximize the return on your investment in the core AX product
- Reduces your development cost and modification footprint
- Avoids modifications which closely resemble standard functionality and may conflict with standard AX functionality

We will now briefly touch on some of the main modules and highlight some of the key areas for consideration.

General Ledger

We've already touched on the most important elements of the G/L in the system-wide section, namely the chart of account and dimensions. It isn't necessary to have defined all the dimension values and validation rules during the initial setup but it is important to decide how many dimensions you will use and whether they are based on other AX tables.

Your decisions on dimensions should influence your chart of accounts design which is very much a G/L setup task. Without G/L accounts in place, posting rules cannot be configured. Without posting rules, many features and functions of modules will not work. For instance, you cannot receive stock, post deliveries, or create invoices. Designing an initial chart of accounts should be top priority in the G/L setup and is likely to be one of the first activities the partner initiates, possibly before all the analysis for the submodules is complete.

Aside from the chart of accounts and dimensional setup, the VAT or Sales Tax functionality is the other major consideration in the G/L module. Dynamics AX has very comprehensive VAT/Sales Tax features, capable of handling the tax systems of many countries. When configured correctly, AX is capable of producing complete VAT or Sales Tax returns, often in a format specific to a country's reporting requirements. AX even has special features to handle part reclamation of tax, for example, on car leases where only 50 percent of the tax charged can be recovered. AX calculates the full tax amount, then deducts the unclaimable portion and posts it to the cost account. This can save a lot of time making offline calculations during invoice posting. AX also stores date ranges against tax rates making it very simple to handle changes in rates, again, providing you have set it up correctly.

In summary, the VAT/Sales Tax functionality is very comprehensive but can appear complicated and overengineered at first. Invest the time early in your project and make sure you understand the business requirements, AX's capabilities and your configuration before going live. Test the tax calculations and reports during the testing phase to ensure that the configuration you have will work once you're live. Remember, when configured correctly, AX will produce your tax return with little to no effort on your part—well worth getting right.

In addition to the core G/L and tax functionality, basic G/L configuration should also include the setup of bank accounts in the bank module. These are linked to appropriate control accounts in the G/L but the use of the bank module in addition to the G/L enables extra functionality such as account reconciliation and the automatic calculation of banking charges.

Fixed assets are also a key part of the finance module although the setup and configuration is usually, fairly, straightforward especially if a well-structured fixed asset register already exists. Unless the financial management of fixed assets is a key priority for the project, the analysis and configuration is typically left until later in the project, once the finance team has completed setup and testing of the core financial features and has the time to invest.

Sales ledger

The sales ledger contains features specific to customers and sales order processing. Most of the configuration in the module will be very specific to the business processes and individual requirements and will be completed by the partner. However, there are some base data tables that need to be set up and giving consideration to them early will avoid making rushed decisions later when it becomes essential to have them populated.

- **Customer groups**: The customer group can control the G/L posting rules used for customer and stock related G/L transactions (although not often used for this purpose) but in this vein it is more often used to control debt collection profiles and some defaults when creating new customers. The customer group can be a powerful analysis field. When creating customer groups, be aware that separate groups are stored for pricing and discounting, sales representatives, and commission. There are also statistic groups for grouping customers by industry segment. With all this in mind, try to ensure your customer groups give you some analysis not offered by the other groups and don't limit your use simply to posting control.
- **Payment terms**: These are fairly simple to configure in the majority of cases. The only special consideration that should be given is if you operate a Direct Debit collection scheme. In these cases, a rounding function which, having calculated the due date based on the payment terms, can then round forwards to a specific day or date, can be very useful for ensuring that collections do not get planned for weekends or in advance of the date agreed with a customer.
- **Methods of payment**: The setup is straightforward (aside from half hidden buttons to set up the file formats), the key overlooked feature is the Bank Transaction Type. Setting this correctly provides better analysis in the Bank module and also when performing a Bank Reconciliation. Although the form is identical, the methods of payment list is maintained separately for the sales ledger and a purchase ledger.

Purchase ledger

The purchase ledger contains features specific to suppliers and purchase order processing. Like the sales ledger, a lot of the configuration in this module will be specific to each implementation, so there are not so many global settings we can discuss without knowledge of the project. Consider the following:

- Give equal consideration to supplier groups as you did to customer groups. Try to think about the kind of analysis you might want to perform later.
- Configure payment terms correctly and if you perform supplier payments on a certain day of the week or date of the month, consider using the rounding feature to round the due date correctly. This will improve the accuracy of cash-flow forecasting reports and allow you to quote accurate payment dates to suppliers when they ask.

- Put effort into obtaining accurate base data for your suppliers, for example address, contact details, bank details, account number, and credit limit. AX will store all this data and it can be used to improve supplier communications and allow reporting and warnings if you stray outside your trading terms.
- Methods of payment—as per the sales ledger; be aware of the often overlooked feature of the Bank Transaction Type.

Product management

Product management and stock management have been separated in AX 2012 to provide additional functionality around using the same items in multiple companies. For the purpose of this book, we will consider the following points to be across product information management and stock management, but the configuration options covered will be found across the two modules.

For product-based businesses, the setup of items will be a major part of the project and there are many options, both in parameters and on the items themselves, that will need to be set. Before you can use any of the order processing, manufacturing, or stock features, you will need to create some items. Rather than talk about the generic properties of these modules, we will highlight a few of the key considerations when deciding how to structure items in Dynamics AX:

- **Units**: Dynamics AX has very flexible unit of measure functionality that allows products to be purchased, stocked, consumed, and sold in different units. The units and conversion between units is configured in the stock management module. It is a good idea to set up all the standard units you might use, and the conversions between them, early in the project. Make sure you:
    - Use accurate descriptions and the correct unit indicators.
    - Set the number of decimal places appropriately for the values you will be entering. Note, if the number of decimal places configured for the unit is less than the number you enter or import, AX will round the value without warning the user.
    - Where possible, set conversion factors between units to enable more flexible item transacting.

> **You only get one chance!**
>
> There are certain fields held against an item that you can't change once transactions have been posted. The stocking unit is a great example. Once you've posted a transaction against an item, the default stocking unit cannot be changed. This unit dictates the unit in which the stock balance is displayed by default so if you get it wrong, you'll spend the rest of your life toggling the balance into another unit every time you want to see it.
>
> The product type can only be set at creation (Item or Configurable Item), which allows variants to be configured. You should also pay particular attention to storage and tracking methods of the item; once transacted upon it is very difficult to add or remove a tracking dimension (that is, Serial Number) or storage dimension (that is, Pallet).

- **Tracking and storage dimensions**: Storage and tracking dimensions are split in this release of AX. Storage dimensions pertain to the physical location of the items (Site, Warehouse, Location, and Pallet). Tracking dimensions pertain to batch and serial numbering. In order to use advanced warehousing features (put away, and so on) the pallet dimension is required, but adds a transaction overhead. Be careful, also, when deciding on batch and serial numbers; only use these if tracking is required within AX (again there is a transactional overhead)—it is not possible to remove after the item has been transacted on, and difficult to add later.
- **Attributes**: New in AX 2012 is the ability to store extended attributes against items without having to create new fields. This uses a new extensible table system and an attribute hierarchy to dictate which attributes apply to different items. This new functionality is in its infancy and doesn't yet support all of the search and selection features you might expect; however, it is a very solid base structure in which to store additional product information. If you plan on storing extended information about your items for a catalog or website consider using this functionality. Make the choice early in the project as configuring the attributes, values, and structures can take a considerable amount of time. Writing import routines to populate the attributes will also require more development than just loading the items.

- **Groups**: There are many groups held against items that control different parts of the stock management and financial postings. The number of groups you create will largely depend on the different configurations you need to support, for example, Items that need serial number tracking will be grouped differently to those that don't. Items to be valued based on FIFO will be grouped differently to those valued using Standard Costing. For certain items you may want to allow physically negative stock, others you may not. All these decisions need to be made, and the information gathered during the analysis, combined with some workshops, should be sufficient to do this. Understanding how AX stock management works early on dramatically improves the chances of building a configuration that works and delivers both the operational and financial functionality required. Making the decisions early on gives you a lot more testing time and opportunity to make revisions and adjustments to this important and complex configuration.

Human resources and users

The HR module of Dynamics AX is used to store information about the employees and contractors who work for your company. This is different to the users table which stores a relationship between Active Directory user accounts and an AX user's ID, in order to grant access to the system. Certain features of AX require a further link between the user and the employee so that they can record which employee or contractor performed an action. A good example is Journal Approval, where a user must be mapped to an employee in order to be able to approve journals.

Until AX 2012, most of the advanced functionality had to be licensed separately, as did the total number of employees, and so the HR module was often used for nothing more than creating the necessary link to a user. With 2012's new licensing model, the full functionality of the HR module is available with no additional license fee. It is therefore worth giving consideration to using the AX HR module in place of existing HR systems. Some benefits of doing this are:

- **Integrated single system**: It reduces the number of separate software systems and databases in use within the business.
- **More value from your investment**: Making more use of the core AX application you purchased.
- **Skills management**: The skills, training, experience, and qualifications stored in AX can be used in other AX modules to help allocate staff with the right skills to tasks and activities. This information can also be used for automated resource planning.

- **Employee self service**: AX's web-based interface, Enterprise Portal, includes an employee section that allows employees to manage and maintain the details held in HR.

Unless HR was a specific requirement when purchasing AX, it is unlikely that the HR module will be considered a critical path or even be included in the requirements analysis beyond providing the basic records required to use certain features in AX. Given that the function AX provides for recruitment, management, and utilization of Human Resources is now quite comprehensive and is already included in the license fee, it makes sense to allocate some time and resources up front to investigate the merits of implementing the module more fully. If this is done early enough in the project, there is usually enough time to allocate some additional client-side resource, normally from HR, to take responsibility for the module's implementation without impacting the main project deliverables.

Summary

In this chapter we have discussed some of the more basic and perhaps often overlooked elements of AX setup. All too often these areas are quickly configured to allow other more important and interesting functionality to be used. The intention is return to these areas later, but time constrains and workloads later in the project preclude the possibility of revisiting these "nice to have" features, given that they are basically configured and not preventing the system from working.

By starting to consider these topics at an early stage of the project, when it seems like there is much more time and resource available, you have the opportunity to configure these base structures and features correctly as well as spending time cleaning the data you plan to import. The majority of the modular setup will be done by or in collaboration with the Partner, who should guide your thinking and make recommendations as to the best way to configure AX. Taking the time to fully understand the features and functionality being configured, and the effect they will have on your use of Dynamics AX, will reduce the chances of having to go back and change the configuration later because the implications of the decision were not fully understood.

In the next chapter, we will cover integration requirements, including the identification and assessment of integration requirements, decisions regarding technology as well as the planning and testing of integrations.

7
Integration

Almost every AX deployment will require some form of integration with third-party software systems. As integration typically requires some development, it is often not analyzed or considered until the specification and development phase. At this point, the emphasis is usually on the technical implementation of the integration rather than the practicalities of operation and the mechanisms for testing.

In our experience, producing an integration plan early in the project, specifically to address all potential integration requirements for the project, helps to ensure that the development, testing, and operating requirements of integration are comprehensively understood, which increases the likelihood of success at go-live.

The following sections discuss the steps required to produce an integration plan, that will ultimately form part of the solution design, and will introduce some of the features and technologies available in AX that can be used to achieve integration between systems.

The main topics discussed in this chapter include:

- Identifying integration
- Accessing integration
- Technologies
- Planning
- Testing

Identifying integration

The first task in creating the integrations plan is to identify all the potential requirements for integration. There are many types of integration ranging from simple file imports and exports, to fully synchronous communication via web services.

Start by making a list of all the applications that Dynamics AX could be required to interact with, and use that as the start of your list of integration points. This list should include every application AX will exchange information with, no matter how trivial. Even exporting data from AX into a flat file to be uploaded into another system or website should be included, provided it is something that will occur more than once in live operation, otherwise it can be considered a data migration activity.

When compiling the list, the integrations can be split into three broad categories:

- **Current integration**: Applications that are currently integrated with the system that AX is replacing. Theoretically, these should be the simplest to implement, as they are already operational and the same integration method might be reused by AX (although if the communication technology used is particularly old, the integration may become more complex).
- **Transition integration**: If the transition between your current system and AX doesn't involve a complete migration of all in-progress transactions at the point of go-live, it is likely that there will be a transition period during which orders or projects run-down in the old system and ramp-up in AX. Consider whether it will be necessary to integrate these systems during this transition period, for example, importing the financial postings into AX for invoices generated in your old system.
- **New integration**: Often one of the main objectives in implementing a new ERP system is to integrate previously disconnected systems. New integration requirements typically require the most planning and design as they do not form part of the current business process or system feature set.

When compiling the list, try to identify and include the following details for each potential integration point, and include them in the integration plan:

- **Software or hardware vendor**: This should include contact details for technical and commercial contact.
- **Version and edition of the system currently in use**: Also identify whether a newer version is available and what upgrade rights or support contracts are in place.
- **Operating system or platform**: Identify where the system runs and whether or not its supporting infrastructure will be affected by your ERP project. For example, does the system run on a server or platform you are trying to decommission as part of the ERP project?
- **Functional description**: Briefly describe what the system does, who it is used by, and for what purpose.
- **Integration requirement**: Identify why the system might be considered for integration with AX and what form that integration might take.

This list will be the basis for the analysis and design activities associated with any system integration, so it is important to ensure that it is comprehensive. Once complete, it is time to assess whether integration will be necessary.

Accessing integration

Having created a list of all the possible integration requirements, we must now assess where integration is necessary and, if so, how it should be implemented. When creating a list of *all* possible system integration points, you will identify application links which will be impractical or unnecessary to implement. There could also be integration proposals whose cost of development will far outweigh the saving in time or cost achieved through integration. The aim is to determine the value of the integration to the business. Use the following tests to assess the list of identified integration opportunities to determine their business value:

- **Data volume**: Is there a high volume of information passed between the two systems? If so, confirm that integration will be quicker and more accurate than data entry.
- **Data integrity**: Are there problems with the accuracy of information exchanged or is the type of information not suitable for manual entry?
- **Real-time feedback**: Is there a requirement to lookup or calculate a value from an external system and display or use it in AX, for example, address lookup from postal/zip code?
- **Process automation**: Is there a requirement to replace a manual process with an automated one, removing the need for user intervention?
- **Data integration**: Is there a requirement to centralize data in a single system for visibility and reporting?

In addition to the drivers for integration, it is important to consider the lifespan of the target application itself. Could the functions it provides be performed by AX, with some development or adaptation? If so, consideration should be given to modifying AX to replace the functions of the third-party application and thus render integration unnecessary. Initially, this approach may cost more than the integration, however, the long term costs in terms of maintaining and supporting the third-party system and its underlying platform products needs to be taken into account especially if the application in question runs on an older platform or hardware that is no longer covered by mainstream support.

If the third-party application will definitely remain, and not be replaced by AX, what is its expected life span, that is how long do you expect it to remain in use? Are any alternatives being considered or are there major version upgrades in the planning that would render the integration obsolete and require significant rework. The effort involved in the design, development, and testing of integrations can be significant and it is very important to make sure that the investment is made with payback before the integration becomes obsolete.

Having assessed the reasons for integration, the next step is to determine the practicality and maturity of the requirement. The combination of these two steps will help you to decide whether or not an integration will be included as part of the solution. To determine the practicality, we need to consider the technological and process options open to us.

Technologies

Dynamics AX offers many options for application integration which makes it possible to integrate with almost any other system. Your selection of integration method should be based on the interface options supported by the other application and the purpose of the integration. For example, if your requirement is to query an external system and display the result to the user in AX, it would be best to use a near real-time integration method like web services, rather than one that relies on batch processes such as file transfer. The following is a high-level list of the integration options Dynamics AX 2012 supports. Use these in conjunction with information on the other system to determine the right technology for development of the integration:

- **Web Service API**: The most "technologically advanced" and robust method of integration, AX exposes many common functions as web service methods via its **Application Integration Framework** (**AIF**). AX also has the facility to make web service calls via the AIF and directly in application code.
- **.Net APIs**: Within AX, it is possible to reference and use APIs that are written and exposed in Microsoft .NET. It is also possible to access COM APIs (pre-.NET) by first wrapping the legacy DLL in .NET. It is also possible to access AX from other applications using the same method (known as the .NET Business Connector) but this feature is deprecated and wherever possible, the Web Service API should be used in preference to the Business Connector.

- **File transfer**: One of the most common integration methods, file transfers, commonly known as CSV, fixed width, and XML files, are a widely used method of integration. File transfers are typically used for one-way communication, for example exporting electronic payments or importing price lists. AX has functions for reading and writing these files directly or via the AIF. While this method is often popular and is sighted as being "simple", building reliable unattended file transfer integrations can be difficult and requires careful thought and planning to ensure graceful handling of errors when one or both sides fail. Typically, web services should be used in preference.
- **Direct database access**: AX has the ability to directly read from and write to other applications' databases if they run on Microsoft SQL Server, or any other database platform provided there is an ODBC or .NET provider. Similarly, other applications capable of reading Microsoft SQL Server databases can be granted direct access to the Dynamics AX database, however, this access should be read only—no application other than AX should ever write to the AX database. This is because AX has many features specifically designed to manage security, consistency, and integrity of data within the database. Allowing applications other than AX to write directly to the database will bypass these checks and could lead to corruption of data or compromise security.

Wherever possible, you should try and use the AIF for all integration between other applications and AX. Using the framework carries an overhead in the initial development and setup of integration but simplifies and eases their operation.

You can modify the core services exposed by the AIF as well as create your own services for custom functionality. The web services are created and exposed using the **Windows Communication Foundation** (**WCF**) which allows a choice of communication (transport) protocols including HTTP and TCP. There is even a filesystem adapter that allows a batch process to pickup files and push them through the services. XSLT or C# transforms can be written to manipulate any data (either in or out of AX) into a format compatible with the AIF methods, allowing it to be used for integration with applications that don't support variable XML schemers or XML at all (for example, those that use CSV).

> **Synchronous communication**
>
> Although the AIF purports to have a "synchronous" mode, this still relies on—certainly for messages originating from AX—a batch trigger and queuing system to process messages and therefore may not be suitable for some operations that require near real-time or continuous communication.

When choosing the technology, be sure to balance the best technological approach with the practicalities of what you are trying to achieve. For example, if you have a tried and tested file-based interface between your current accounting system and your electronic banking software for making payments, there is no need to change to a web service call just because AX supports it. Keep in mind that changing both ends of the integration means more testing and you need to make sure the benefits you gain are worth this increased overhead.

Planning

Having identified all possible integration options, assessed the drivers for and merits of each, and decided how best they can be achieved, you should be in a position to create a definitive list of all integrations that will be delivered as part of your project. The development work should be added to the development plan and handled in the same way as all other modifications - following the same specification, approval, and development procedures. However, there are a few extra points to consider when developing an integration:

- **Documentation**: Make sure you provide as much documentation about the target system's integration capabilities as possible and have this available during the analysis, design, and development phases.
- **Upgrades**: Establish whether there will be any major changes or upgrades to the application between the time you write the specification, develop the software, and go-live. If you are not currently using the latest version of a product, establish the features and benefits that upgrading to the current version would bring, and whether or not it affects the way you approach the integration.
- **Data Mapping**: Consider whether key fields and references are consistent between systems or whether mapping and translation will be required. AX has a built-in framework for storing "external references" which can be used to store these mapping values, but this needs to be taken into account at the specification stage and the data setup will need to be done before testing can take place.
- **External parties**: If the integration is between your AX system and an external party (for example, customer or supplier), the design, specification, and development process may need to be coordinated with them. Be sure to involve them as soon as is practical to make sure they can work to your time scales.

- **Security**: Consider the security context the integration will operate in and the requirements in AX, the target application and in underlying platforms such as Windows, Unix, SQL Server, and so on. As discussed earlier, data being brought into AX must pass through the AX application to be validated and inserted correctly. Also ensure that the integration cannot unknowingly be used to bypass security in either application, for example users are prevented from editing the data in AX but find that they can change it in the system it was sent to.
- **Resources**: It may be necessary to have users with experience or knowledge of the third-party system available during the processes, especially during the testing phase. Ensure you have identified these people in advance and that they are prepared to be involved and available when required.

Testing

Once the development is complete, as with all modifications, you will need to perform testing. Testing integration is not as straightforward as testing modifications that only affect the AX application. It is important to give consideration as to how and to what extent you will test the integration before and after go-live as early in your project as possible, so that you can ensure the necessary environments and resources are available. When integrating with systems outside your organization, for example customers, suppliers, or banks, start liaising early to find out if there are any constraints or limiting factors at their end that will affect your ability to test your software.

The amount of testing and the form it will take will vary depending on the type of systems being integrated, whether the integration is new or has been used before and who will be expected to use it. The following sections highlight some of the key considerations when planning integration testing.

Test environments

While it is common to have multiple AX environments for live operation, testing, and development, this is not typically true of all business applications. Consider how you will test your integration without these environments or plan to provision a test system before the developments are complete. If you plan to test against a live system, make sure your test scripts won't create data that could interfere with live operations. Ensure you have a method for clearing out the test records.

> **Testing with the AIF**
>
> For integrations that use the AIF, a considerable amount of configuration is held in metadata which will have to be recreated in each environment. In our experience, changes made during testing can be easily missed and thus we have found it better to configure the AIF elements in LIVE and then copy the environment to TEST. Amendments to configuration should be made in LIVE and then the environment should be copied again for testing. We have found this the best way to avoid issues in LIVE.

During your assessment of environments, it is important to consider any middleware that might be involved in the integration process, for example file transfer scripts. Consider how these will work in a test scenario and what amendments, if any, will be required in live operation.

Resourcing

Unlike modifications which only affect functionality inside AX, the developers may not be able to perform extensive testing of integration code without access to and knowledge of the target system. As such, plan for a higher testing workload for client-side resources that have experience of the target system. You may need to involve additional parties in the testing phase including AX consultants and/or consultants from the target application supplier. The level of resource and involvement in testing will depend on the complexity and nature of the integration. For example, testing an electronic payment export to a banking system will probably only require the purchase ledger clerk who normally processes payments and won't necessitate hiring personnel from your bank. Conversely, a tight two-way integration between AX and a production control system will almost certainly require input from consultants and developers from the production control system provider. Factor in additional time for rework after the initial round of testing and ensure that you have appropriate resources available to test end-to-end functionality not just the technical implementation of the integration.

Scope of testing

Consider to what extent the integration must be tested. For example, an electronic payments file that is imported and validated by banking software before being transmitted to the bank only needs to be tested as far as import and validation on the assumption that if this passes, the submission to the bank will be successful. Ensure that your test plans go far enough to validate the integration without committing you to unnecessary testing of the functions of third-party applications already known to be working.

Summary

Integration between systems is often cited as one of the key drivers for the implementation of AX. When done correctly, integration can provide massive productivity gains by reducing error and improving the flow of information between systems. Identifying integration opportunities early in the project is one of the best ways to guarantee success. Creating an integration plan helps to ensure that you identify all the possible integration options and assess how and why they should be implemented. The integration plan also draws together all the information and documentation that will be needed, well in advance, for the analysis, design, and development phases, helping to reduce delays and ensure that modifications are delivered on time. Finally, it allows you to plan the testing activities and identify the resources and systems you need well in advance should any additional setup or installation be required.

In *Chapter 8, Harnessing the Power of Standard AX Features*, we will discuss the benefits of standard AX and how to harness the power of standard features by utilizing workflow, advanced filters, cues, alerts, personalization, and security.

8

Harnessing the Power of Standard AX Features

In the last chapter, we focused on identifying integrations between AX and other systems and how they might be achieved through development and customization. Later we'll be looking at the modification and development process required to fill the gaps identified during the Diagnostic phase, but in this chapter we focus on the wealth of standard functionality in AX and how it can be used to change and improve processes without development.

The main topics discussed in this chapter include:

- Workflow
- Advanced filters
- Cues
- Alerts
- Personalization

Understanding Workflow in AX

The term "workflow" is used heavily in AX projects. People often refer to business processes as workflows, for example, sales order processing as "the sales order workflow" however it is important to differentiate between this use of the word and what constitutes a workflow in AX.

In AX terms, a workflow is a sequence of actions executed at specific points in the standard software, the behavior of which can be controlled through configuration rather than development. Put simply, by implementing workflows, Microsoft has moved the "business logic" of some AX processes from code, editable by developers, to data, editable by super users, typically from the IT or IS team. This has several advantages:

- The business logic of a process can be defined and edited by a super-user rather than a developer, which often removes the need to involve external resources from the partner, saving time and money.
- There is no impact on the code, which means no development footprint and no code upgrade issues when upgrading between service packs and versions (although the workflow configuration data will have to be upgraded, this should be handled by standard upgrade routines provided by Microsoft).
- Developing new workflows in AX 2012 will also have a reduced footprint compared to modifying core AX functionality; the configuration data for these workflows *should* be taken care of by the data upgrade features in the next release of AX.
- Workflows are version controlled and each instance of a workflow knows the version that was active when it was started. This allows changes to workflows to be planned and will not cause workflows that are in progress to break.
- The logic is held in data and can be written to act on data, allowing decision blocks to be built based on values held in setup tables, for example item group or customer group. When writing business logic in code, it is bad practice to develop based on values held in data that could change (imagine if you deleted or renamed a customer group) but the workflow engine is specifically designed to handle these situations gracefully.

Dynamics AX 2012 provides a good number of standard workflows out of the box; these can be used by enabling them from the forms found in the setup section of each module and defining the workflow logic using the graphical workflow designer, another new addition to AX 2012. These standard workflows are most commonly used to handle the approval of standard business documents, for example purchase requisitions or expenses claims, and allow a very granular level of system based control that would normally be too expensive to develop in code. The graphical workflow designer enables a super-user to define a process through which a document or transaction must pass to be approved. The workflow engine can evaluate data stored in AX and use decision blocks to route the document down the required path. Let's look at a simple purchase requisition approval process as an example.

First we need to establish the business rules for approval and check that they can be modeled and evaluated in AX. In our example, these are all based around the total value of the requisition:

- If the value is between 0 and 1,000 GBP - automatically approve
- If the value is between 1,000 and 5,000 GBP - send to purchasing manager who can approve
- If the value is greater than 5,000 GBP - send to purchasing manager for first approval then send to all directors any one of whom can provide the second approval; which can be done in parallel
- If an employee is on holiday, delegate to a colleague for a predefined period
- Based on a manual decision (when purchasing a "special" item, request that the user decides on the next branch in the workflow, that is who to send it to)
- Once approved, automatically perform a task, that is "post requisition"
- Should the workflow take too long to approve, trigger an escalation or return it to its originator

This is a very simple example of a workflow but it illustrates how AX can evaluate the subject of a workflow and use other data held in the system, in this case employees and groups, to route messages and control who can approve transactions.

Using Workflow to its full potential

The AX Workflow engine has more capabilities than the standard workflows take advantage of; for instance, you can have check list tasks that need to be marked as complete before the approval can be completed.

You may want to create an item creation approval where several groups of people are responsible for parts of the item creation (Sales, Purchasing, Warehousing, and so on). In this scenario, you would have a check list for each group of stakeholders.

For more information on workflow checklists see MSDN: `http://msdn.microsoft.com/en-gb/library/cc620991.aspx`

There are limitations as to what workflow can do and it is certainly not as powerful and flexible as writing custom code to manage a process, however, workflows offer improved maintainability, reduced cost of implementation and maintenance, and more flexible criteria (such as, the ability to use table values). There may be situations where the features of the workflow engine would satisfy a requirement but no standard workflow is available. To address this, the workflow framework has been made available to developers so that new workflows can be developed for standard AX functions or as part of custom modifications. Once the "hook" into the process has been added in code, the logic of the workflow is defined using the graphical workflow designer in the same way as the standard ones.

> **Custom workflows**
>
> Note that unlike the standard workflows that are included as part of AX 2012, additional custom workflows developed specifically for an implementation do carry a small code footprint and therefore have an impact during upgrades. This is preferable, where appropriate, to modifying standard AX functionality as the code footprint is typically smaller; business rules are held in configuration data rather than code; and changes to the rules are fully version controlled.

Taking the time to understand the standard workflows that are included in Dynamics AX, where they are triggered and what they can control, should be your starting point for assessing if and how they can be used in your deployment. Microsoft has made a significant investment in workflow in AX 2012, most notably in the graphical workflow designer and the number of standard workflows included, giving a clear indication that they believe, where possible, workflow should be used to model processes rather than changes to code.

Although the workflow capabilities of AX 2012 can be considered very good and a big improvement on previous versions, they are not yet so advanced that all business logic and processes can be modeled using them. The performance dictated by the inherently asynchronous nature of the workflows is one of the most limiting factors, meaning that you can't prompt a user for feedback while they are in a form, making it unsuitable for many of the rules you might add to the Sale Order form for example. Keeping these limitations in mind, try to use workflows for processes that do not require real-time interaction or feedback and require involvement from more than one user. Approvals are a great example of this as is the setup of base data such as items and products.

If you decide to use workflows as part of your solution, we recommend you create a workflow plan that details where the workflows will be used and who will be responsible for their design, implementation, testing, and maintenance. If you plan to develop new workflows not included in standard AX, make sure they are specified and developed as part of the Development phase, and that you leave sufficient time for configuration and testing after the code delivery.

Advanced filters

The methods of searching and filtering will become very familiar to users as they start working with AX. However, it is possible to overlook just how powerful the advanced filter capabilities of AX can be especially when coupled with favorites and cues (discussed in more detail later in the chapter). The advanced filter screen in AX is available from every list page and form, and allows the user to build up a more complicated filter involving multiple fields and tables. The filters can be saved and shared with other users or associated with a favorite to automatically open a form and apply the filter. For example, you could create an advanced filter on the **Main accounts** list page to show only accounts in a certain number range and exclude accounts of type **Total**, then save the filter as **Sales Accounts**:

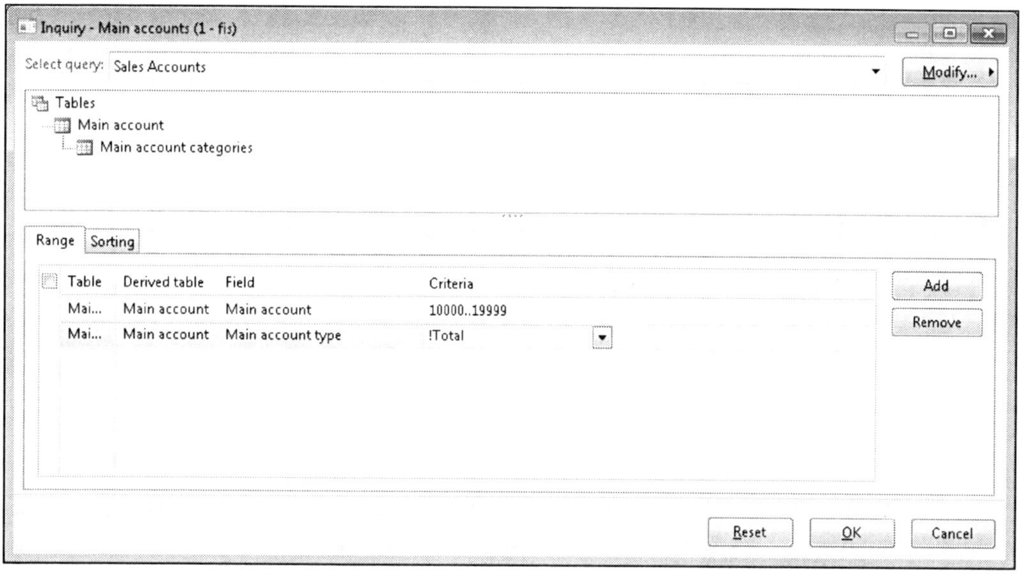

When adding the **Main accounts** shortcut to your favorites, you'll be offered the option of choosing a saved filter. If you select **Sales Accounts** you will have effectively created a button that just displays the sales accounts in the chart of accounts. Imagine how powerful this can be if users are trained to use this feature properly. They can effectively build their own mini-menu structure that automatically filters the screen to show the information they need. Cues take this concept one stage further and will be discussed in the next section.

Another often overlooked feature of advanced filters is their ability to join in extra tables. Because AX knows the relationships between its database tables, it is able to offer users the option of including related tables in the filter. A great example is adding customer transactions to the customer list so you can filter the list to only include customers who have bought something in say, the last year.

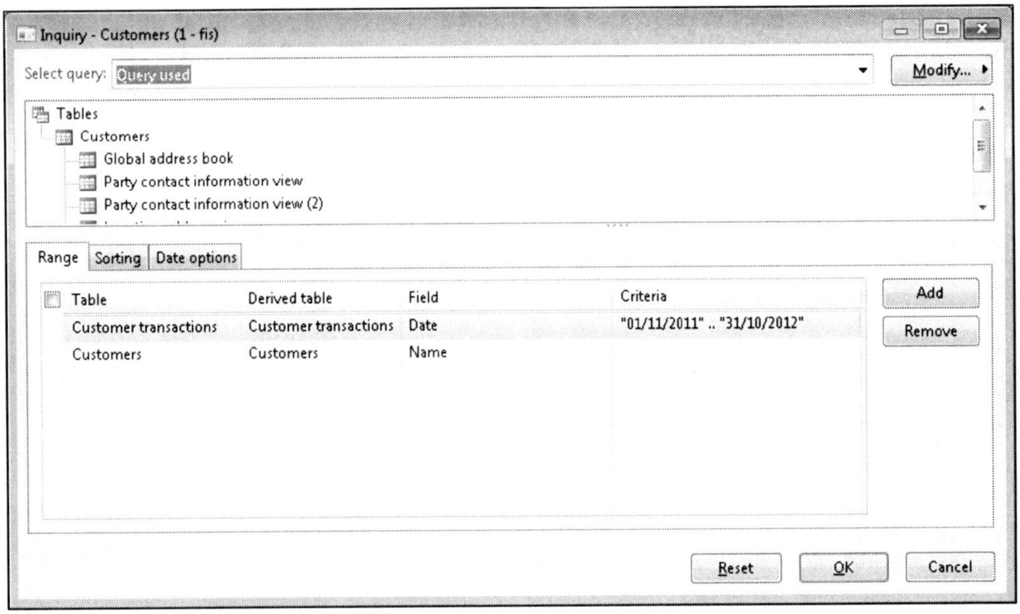

You could then send the filtered list of customers to Excel and use it to perform a mail merge, all without any development input.

Filtering in AX

AX lets you use several operators in the criteria in filters. In the previous example, the range operator " .. " was used to create a filter between date X and date Y. Other operators such as " * ", a wild card, for example "Smith*" would return anything beginning with Smith; and " , " which allows you to list multiple criteria, for example "CUST101, CUST107, CUST289", which would just return those specific accounts. For full details of all the search operators supported in AX 2012 with examples, see the following TechNet article: `http://technet.microsoft.com/en-us/library/aa569937.aspx`.

Cues

Cues were first introduced in AX 2009 when list pages first made an appearance. A cue is a visual representation, on the user's role center, of a count of records from a list page that meet specific criteria. They are used to provide a quick visual indication of the volume of work at a particular status then give the user a single-click drill-down to the list page showing just the relevant records. When used correctly, they provide users with a highly tailored view of information, directing their attention to priorities and providing quick navigation to filtered list pages. Because they can be created and added to role centers without development, they can be considered a configuration activity which, when done correctly, can provide users with a very personal, role tailored interface to Dynamics AX.

There are many predefined cues in standard AX as well as the ability to define new cues during development or even at an end-user level. User defined cues can be personal or can be shared system-wide with other users.

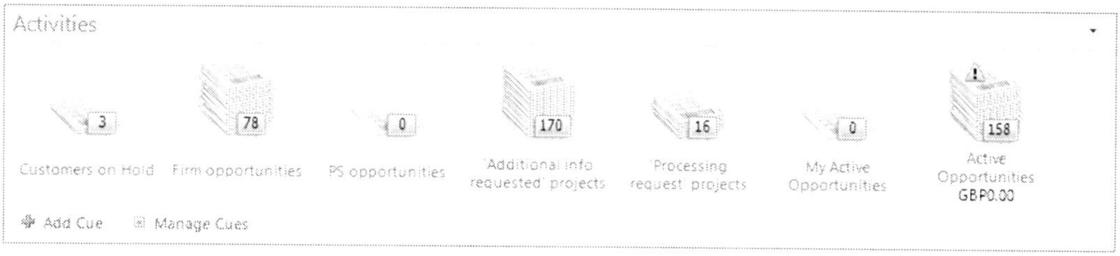

Creating a user-defined cue

A very simple example would be a cue showing the number of customers on hold. To create a cue, you first need to filter a list page to show the records you want to build the cue count on. For our example, we need to filter the customer list page to show only those customers on hold. AX 2012 has this filter and cue predefined. First, navigate to: **Sales Ledger** | **Common** | **Customers** | **Customers on Hold**. Clicking on the list page title (the green text in the upper-left corner) gives us access to the list page options from which we can set or edit the filter applied to the list page and choose to **Save as cue**.

When saving the cue, we can specify the following:

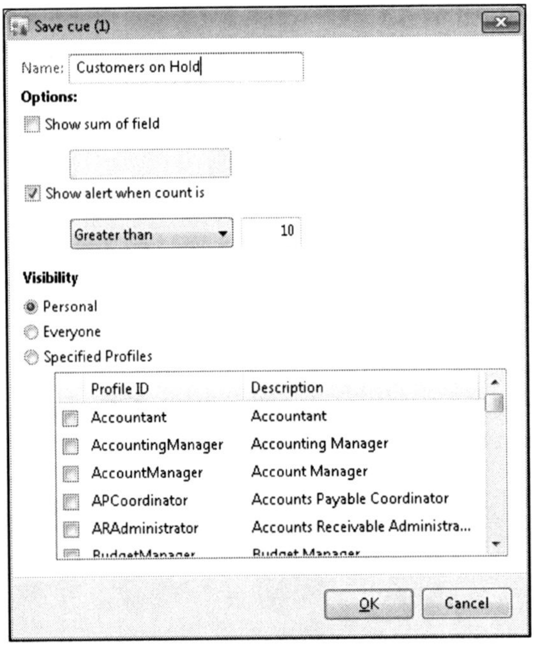

- **Name** - this will appear on the role center as the label for the cue. Because it is user definable, it can be set to something that makes sense to the user and is in keeping with the company's terminology.
- **Show sum of field** - this option sums a field from the table and display it under the cue icon on the role center. An example might be to total the value of unapproved purchase requisitions, for example 32 unapproved purchase requisitions, £56,762.90.
- **Show alert when count is** - based on the count of records, we can set a point at which a yellow warning triangle will be displayed over the icon. This is an excellent visual cue for users to address the most urgent priorities.
- **Visibility** - specifies who can see the cue.

Understanding how cues work and implementing them will help you provide a rich role tailored user interface, aligned to the business, with no (or with very little) custom development. Plan cues, role centers, and security as part of the same activity as they are all based around user roles. Try to start this early enough so that a version is available for the UAT phase, and you have time to make changes and adjustments before going live. These role centric tasks are often left as a post go-live activity and are then rarely implemented, which is a shame given how powerful and helpful correctly configured cues can be.

Alerts

Alerts were first introduced in AX 4.0 and have changed very little since then. Quite simply, they give the user the ability to configure an alert that notifies them, via a pop up in AX or an e-mail, when a change is made to a record or field in a table or when a date becomes or passes due. Alerts are created by right-clicking on a record and choosing **Create alert rule...**.

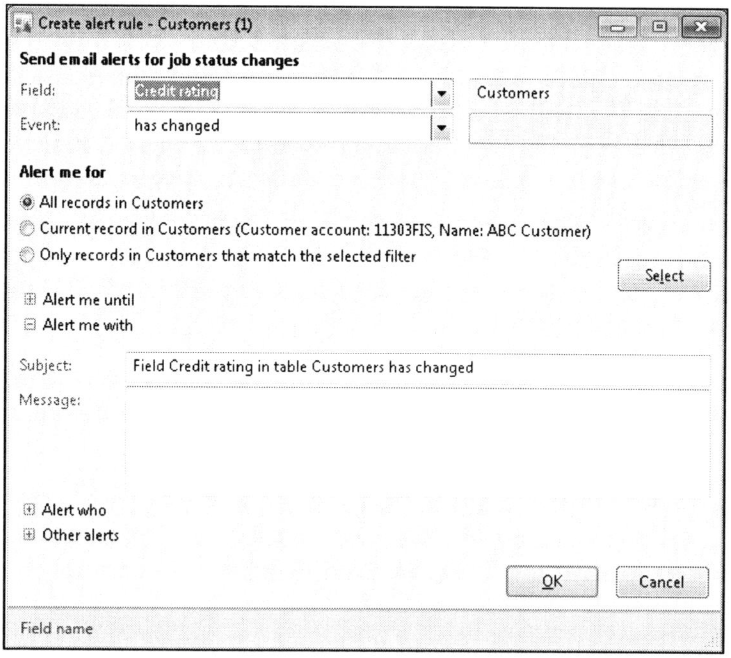

The alert rule setup form allows us to specify criteria and conditions that should trigger the rule as well as the message that will appear in the alert.

- Field level alerts are used to monitor changes to an individual field, such as the credit rating, and can be triggered when any change is made or when the field is set to a specific value. For example, the sales manager might wish to be alerted when any change is made to any customer's credit limits (use event: "has changed"), but only wish to be told when an account is placed on invoice hold (use event: "is set to" and select a value).
- All field alerts monitor the table for creation or deletion of records. For example, the warehouse manager may wish to be alerted when a new product is added to AX.

The scope of an alert can also be configured to further reduce the number of messages received:

- All records in table - the rule will execute for any record in the specified table.
- Current record in table - always shows the record you right-clicked on to open the alert form. It can be useful if you want to monitor a specific customer or item for example.
- Only records in table that match the selected filter - this is used in combination with the standard AX filter screen and allows you to specify a custom filter that will be used to trigger the rule. A good example is using a filter to select only the customers where you are assigned as the "Employee Responsible", so that you only receive alerts about your customer accounts.
- Alert me until - allows us to specify an end date for the rule or just let it run until we disable it. This can be useful when you only want to monitor something for a seasonal event, for example a particularly fast moving product line at Christmas.

Finally we can set the subject and message and who will be alerted. Typically this is the user performing the set up but it is possible to specify a different user, for example if a manager is setting up an alert for an employee.

When working with date-based alerts, the rules can be configured to trigger when a specific date is reached or changed. This can be useful for alerting when a sales order passes its delivery date without being marked as delivered, for example.

There is sometimes confusion as to the overlap between workflow and alerts, and which is best to use. As a guide workflow, when available, should be used to manage a process where:

- the path will be determined by multiple decisions or criteria
- involves multiple people
- spans a period of time
- needs tracking to ensure it is not forgotten

Alerts can only act on real data and cannot perform calculations like totaling sales order lines and sending an alert when an order passes a certain value. This is a good example of when a workflow would be more appropriate.

Alerts should be used to notify a single user about a specific event. They are not capable of managing a process or notifying multiple users.

Alerts are most useful not for managing processes but rather for dealing with exceptions. Well configured personal alerts can be used to help users monitor AX activity and identify events that may need attention. An example could be an account manager setting an alert that tells him when a sales order is entered for a new customer, for the first month of trading, so that he can call the customer and check if everything was satisfactory. Another example might be the warehouse manager setting an alert so that they are notified when an order, for a customer who has complained about the packing of their recent order, enters the picking process, so that they can personally check the order before it is dispatched. These are just two very common scenarios which are often handled through free text notes against a customer account or order, which rely on users reading them and taking action. The use of alerts means the right people are notified automatically without any action from users and that important tasks outside of the normal workflow are handled correctly.

Personalization

Personalization is a feature of AX, previously known as form setup, which allows a user to personalize the look and feel of AX forms and lists. Personalization is often demonstrated during the presales process, highlighting the simplicity with which forms can be changed, as a major selling point of AX over other systems. While personalization is a powerful and useful feature and can have many benefits when used correctly, it can also be a source of problems and confusion if used in the wrong way or at the wrong time.

Understanding the capabilities of personalization

We'll start by looking at what can be achieved using personalization. The personalization form offers the user control over the layout, labeling and behavior of the fields and buttons on forms.

> Note that personalization is specific to the user and cannot be used to affect all users of AX.

Like filters, personalization settings that have been saved can be retrieved and loaded by other users, but there is no facility to apply these to groups or all users.

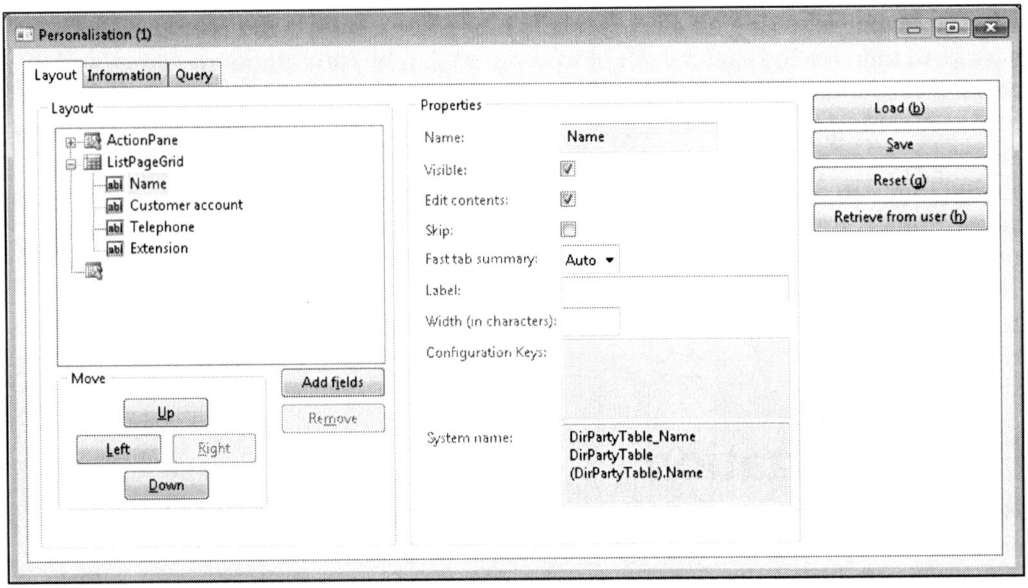

The tree view on the left-hand side displays a representation of the structure of the form in terms of tabs, groups, grids, and fields or buttons. Selecting a node in the tree allows you to alter some of the properties of that form element, if the developer has allowed it.

- **Visible**: Unchecking this box makes the field or button invisible to the user. AX will redraw the form to use the space that the field or button occupies.
- **Edit contents**: Unchecking this box prevents editing of the field, effectively making it read only.
- **Skip**: When ticked, the field or button is excluded from the tab order (the sequence the cursor moves through when the tab key is pressed) giving the ability to skip past the field or button when navigating the form using the keyboard.
- **Fast tab summary**: It dictates whether the field will be included in the summary section at the top of a fast tab. **No** explicitly removes it from the summary, **Yes** forces it to be included, and **Auto** defers to the behavior specified by the developer.

- **Label**: Allows you to change the label applied to a field or button. For example, you could change the **Name** column on the customer list page to "Customer Name".
- **Width**: Allows you to specify a number of characters the field should be sized to display.

In addition to changing the properties of existing fields and buttons, personalization also gives us the ability to add additional fields to the form as well as change the order and position they are laid out in:

- **Add fields**: Displays a pop up showing all the tables associated with the form and the fields they contain. Choosing a field from the list adds it to the form, in the group or grid that was selected in the tree view control when the **Add fields** button was clicked.
- **Direction buttons**: **Up** and **Down** changes the order in which the field or button selected in the tree view appears in the list. This in turn affects the order in which they appear on the form. **Left** and **Right** moves the selected field or button between groups, and can be used to move fields from one tab or group to another. This is most often used to move fields from tabs onto the overview grid.
- **Drag-and-drop**: It is possible to reposition fields and buttons using drag-and-drop instead of the direction buttons.

Once they have finished editing the form, the user can save their changes and give their specific setup a name. A user can create multiple versions of a personalized form, save them under different names, and then load the one they want.

Personalization versus development

It is clear that the personalization features of Dynamics AX are very powerful and could be used to achieve lots of the form redesign that is commonly asked for by users during implementation, without the need to make development level modifications to AX. The only obvious limitation is that each user has to proactively load the layout from the user that made the changes; however, many decide to live with this limitation if it means getting the form layouts they want without the cost of development. This is a very bad decision to make and we will now explain why.

When users see AX for the first time they are often overwhelmed by the number of fields and buttons available on each screen. Once they learn that AX has features that allow these forms to be changed, the project team is usually inundated with requests for form modifications. The implementation partner will normally take a pragmatic approach to the changes, accepting those that make a functional difference to the system and rejecting those aimed at making forms slightly prettier or easier to use. It is at this point that some companies decide to go down the personalization route to achieve the level of change they believe they require. Before we look at the appropriate use of personalization, let's be clear on its use as a substitute for system-wide development level changes. Quite simply, it isn't. Changes to forms that have a genuine benefit and need to be applied to all users should always be done through development. Personalization should not be used as an economical alternative for all the reasons we are about to discuss.

Using personalization appropriately

Having established that personalization is a powerful end user tool but not a substitute for development, we will now explore its limitations and appropriate use.

When we make changes to forms in the development environment, the changes are stored in the application layers in the same way changes to code and tables are. This is why changes made in development automatically apply to all users. Just like changes to code and tables, changes to a standard AX form in the development environment creates what we call a footprint in a higher layer. Items with a footprint have an impact on upgrades as they have to be compared to the upgraded version to check for and resolve any conflicts. Of all the components of AX that is possible to modify through development, forms are the most time consuming and therefore most costly to upgrade. This explains why partners should discourage nonessential cosmetic changes to forms as each one will increase the time and therefore the cost of upgrade, potentially making it unviable for the client to upgrade in the future.

Personalizations are not stored in the same way as changes made through development and as such don't carry the same upgrade cost because instead of comparing differences between the personalized and upgrade version, more often than not, AX will simply ignore or misapply the personalization. Nine times out of ten when a form is upgraded a user will be forced to delete their personalization, revert to the standard upgraded form before it displays properly. The same is true if the form is changed through development rather than an upgrade. After the user has reverted back to the standard version, if they still need their personalizations, they must recreate them from scratch.

Now that we understand how personalizations differ from development level changes, and under what circumstances they will fail to apply correctly, we can see why making extensive use of personalization may not be a good idea:

- Personalizations are often lost or corrupted when the form is changed through development or upgrade, causing one or more of the following:
    - The user is prevented from seeing the changes made through development or upgrade
    - The form displays incorrectly or not at all
    - The user is forced to wipe out all personalizations and then recreate them in order to get the form to work correctly
- During the months after go-live there is typically ongoing development and bug fixing that will require development changes to forms. Keeping in mind the problems associated with deploying changes to personalized forms, it is likely that users will be forced to delete and recreate their personalizations several times. This often causes them to become annoyed and can damage user confidence in AX.
- When trying to provide support, particularly by telephone or remotely, it can be difficult to establish a common understanding if a user has a heavily personalized form. Imagine telling a user to look for a field which is visible for one user but not for another because it has been hidden or renamed through personalization. It can also make reading and executing standard procedures using process guides difficult if the screen no longer matches the examples provided.

Based on these points, we would advise restricting the use of personalization from the general user base until after the initial "bedding in" phase. Wait until the majority of development and bug fixes are completed and you've stabilized the application to a point where changes are not being deployed on a regular basis. This should coincide with a drop in support requests on how processes work in AX making it less important that support teams and users be working on identical screens.

In summary, personalization is a very powerful and useful feature of AX which when used correctly can increase users' satisfaction with AX and boost their productivity. To help you successfully manage the deployment of personalization we suggest creating a personalization policy that outlines when the facilities will be made available and how they should be used. You can enforce the policy through security by denying users access to the personalization menu option. Denying users access to personalization (via the **Client Essential** security duty) initially has the added benefit of forcing them to report changes to forms that are really necessary for them to do their jobs so that they can be addressed correctly through development, as well as helping to avoid the problems and pitfalls outlined above.

Security

Security is always a hot topic during the implementation of an ERP system. Many projects start out with the aim of defining very tight, almost user specific permissions, but end up giving super user or administrator permissions to nearly everyone shortly after go-live so they can access the features and data they need.

Dynamics AX 2012 introduces a complete new security model compared to previous versions which, as discussed earlier, is based around a user's role rather than the traditional security groups. AX 2012 provides over 80 security roles out of the box which cover roles from "Sales Clerk" to "Accountant" to "Chief Executive Officer". As roles can be added to other roles, one of the best implementation methods, although not applicable to all projects, is to create new roles that reflect your teams, and then add the appropriate standard roles to them. For example, you might decide that your finance team should have access to all the accounting, cost accounting, and product management functions. In this case you would create a new role called "Finance" and add the appropriate standard AX roles (Accountant, Cost accountant, and Product design manager) beneath it. Organizing standard roles into roles that match your organizational structure delivers a usable security setup far quicker than the old granular permissions system of previous versions, but it still doesn't deliver a 100 percent fit. In most cases, it will still be necessary to add individual permissions to your role to grant users all the access they need without giving them access to things that they don't.

> **Don't go to deep!**
>
> When nesting security roles under each other, ensure that your configuration does not go more than 3 levels deep. This is a limit which AX imposes but doesn't validate in the setup form. It will only cause a problem when a developer tries to compile the whole application at which point the compiler will throw an error!

As result of restricting what your users can access, security helps with user interface customization. When you remove a user's access to a field or button through security, AX uses its dynamic form drawing capabilities (known as MorphX) to re-layout the form to fill the gaps left by the removed fields and buttons. The net effect is the same as hiding through personalization or development except that it can be applied to a group of users rather than just one or everyone. You can experience some issues with code moves and upgrades if security has been set up tightly to remove unwanted fields, but because your security should be built around access to menu items and tables, the impact should be minimal and fairly easy to resolve. Well-designed security can help "de-clutter" forms and remove unnecessary menu items without personalization or development. But make sure you don't go too far and remove too much, as more often than not you'll end up moving the users to a higher role to get around the problem—and never move them back again!

Watch out for footprints!

Creating and editing security roles creates entries in the **Application Object Tree** (**AOT**) which is normally only modified by developers. To help keep these security objects separate and minimize the disruption when moving changes from other environments, decide which users will be responsible for creating and managing roles and make sure they are all set to work in the same application layer and model. You should create a specific model just for security and set that as the security administrators default model.

Finally, we need to consider licensing. As we've already discussed, AX 2012 introduces a whole new licensing mechanism based on the type of user rather than modules. AX determines the user type based on the menu items (buttons) the user has access to and *not* the ones they actually use. As such, you'll need to keep in mind when designing your security roles that granting access to certain menu items will push a role into a different category of user and therefore could have a cost implication. There is an AX batch job that runs to make an assessment of users based on their assigned roles called "Named user license count reports processing". Each time this job runs the license assessment data will be updated and the count by user type can be viewed using the report found in **System Administration** | **Reports** | **Licensing** | **Named User Licence Counts**.

The trick to getting security right at go-live is to start early enough so that you have time to implement and test, but not so early that the exact features you'll use and custom developments are not yet complete. Try to do as much planning and investigation of the standard roles as possible before you start implementing your own roles and if possible, get the first version in before UAT, that way you can test your security setup at the same time as the application.

Summary

In this chapter we've learnt how standard features of the AX application can be used to deliver a customized and tailored user experience without the use of development. All these features have the ability to enhance your solution if used correctly and the ability to cause serious problems if used badly. The key to making good use of the standard application is to build an understanding of the features capabilities and limitations, then test the customizations you plan to make to ensure they are adequately accommodated. As all the features discussed are standard, your learning can start as soon as you have a test system available and you don't have to wait until the final solution design and development is complete to start building your knowledge and plan.

Building a knowledge of standard AX and exploring options to meet requirements without modification is an excellent approach to take and will help ensure the developments you do make return maximum value. In our experience, many needless modifications have been performed in the past; either on the assumption that something can't be accomplished as standard, or because the end-user is unwilling to consider a change in process to align it to standard Dynamics AX. A common example of this is logistics and warehousing, where the standard system is far more powerful and capable than many partners and customers realize. This results in modifications such as bespoke sales reservation forms, changes to pallet handling logic, and bespoke inspection and quarantine control systems. In many cases, these can be handled by a mixture of adopting the AX processes and detailed configuration, both of which take time—which is why it is so important to give yourselves adequate time for planning, prototyping, and testing. The more standard functionality you use, the easier and cheaper upgrades will be and the more value you get from your investment in the AX license.

In the next chapter, we will be learning about the Design and Development phases of the implementation, including understanding the impact of change and modifications, understanding the AX architecture, deciding on what to change, and planning the development.

9

Designing and Developing the Solution

In the previous chapter, we focused on getting the most out of some of the standard features of Dynamics AX, and how they can be used to deliver a tailored user experience without the need for development.

Despite the power and flexibility of standard AX, there are some requirements, which can only be met by making changes to the standard application or by developing completely new data structures and code.

We will be examining the development capabilities in Dynamics AX and providing guidance on what should and should not be changed, as modifications form a key part of the solution design. Although not strictly part of the Design phase, we will also discuss the building and testing process and the options for managing the transition of code between environments. As this book's primary purpose is to help you plan, manage, and execute a successful Dynamics AX 2012 project, this chapter will not provide specific guidance on the design and development of modifications in AX. It will however, help you to identify and mitigate some of the major risks associated with configuring and changing Dynamics AX.

The following topics will be covered in this chapter:

- Understanding the impact of change
- Planning the development
- Practical advice for the Development phase
- Managing environments

Understanding the impact of change

By the time a company has made the decision to purchase and implement Dynamics AX, they have usually been introduced to, as part of the pre-sales process, the powerful development capabilities and been shown how easy it is to add new fields or change the appearance of forms. The power of its development capabilities is one of AX's most impressive features and a key differentiator between it and other ERP systems; making a pre-sales demonstration particularly relevant. However, it is important to understand that just because AX can be changed, it doesn't mean it is always the best option. Some of the best AX implementations involve heavy modifications, however some of the worst are the ones where modifications have been designed badly or are used in place of configuration of the standard software. The first key to success is to clearly identify the business or technological case for the change, and to accept or reject that case based on a good understanding of the impact the change will have on:

- Testing and UAT timescales
- Usability
- Performance
- Scalability
- Maintainability
- Hotfixes, service packs, and version upgrades

As is often the case with software development, there are many ways of modifying the AX application to achieve the same functional result. Choosing the right method requires a deep understanding of the standard AX application functionality and how it is implemented at a technical level. The second key to a successful project involving modification is to ensure that the changes you make are correctly designed and implemented.

To fully understand the impact of change, we need to go beyond the basics learnt in the pre-sales demonstration and understand a little bit more about the architecture of Dynamics AX.

Understanding the AX architecture

Dynamics AX has an **Integrated Development Environment** (**IDE**), which allows partners, independent software vendors (ISVs), and the end customer to make changes to the standard application, as well as develop new functionality of their own. Giving all these parties the ability to change and add to the AX application could create a problem in terms of source code maintenance and change tracking; so, AX implements a unique system called **Layers** to help us manage the application code. In AX 2012, a new concept called **Models** was added to the layer architecture.

The layer system was designed to allow separation of developments done by different parties. This separation also helps us to identify and move developments between systems. The term Layers is used because each party's development effectively sits above the previous one overriding the code below.

The base application code for the standard AX functionality, developed and maintained by Microsoft, is held in the core non-editable layer known as the SYS layer. The next layer is known as SYP, which is the patch layer for service packs, hotfixes, and occasionally new functionality that was written after the initial release; this is also released and maintained by Microsoft. For every standard layer, there is a patch layer giving all developers the ability to segregate their code. AX has 16 layers in total, half of which are for patches, which in practice are rarely used by anyone other than Microsoft. From here on, we will only deal with the most commonly used non-patch layers, identified in the following table:

Layer	Purpose	Controlled By
USR	To contain development performed by the customer (that is, system owner) for an individual implementation.	Customer
CUS	To contain development performed by the customer that is system wide or global. Typically only used on global projects.	Customer
VAR	To contain development performed by the partner on behalf of the customer.	Partner
ISV	To contain vertical solutions or add-on's developed by third party ISVs that are installed as part of the solution.	ISV
SYS	To contain the core application and all of Dynamics AX's standard features.	Microsoft

The developer chooses which layer they wish to work in before opening the AX client using the AX Client Configuration Utility. All the layers apart from the USR layer are protected by a password that is individually generated for each layer, for each license. The AX partner will have access to the passwords for all layers from VAR upwards through partner source. Only ISVs will be able to access the ISV layer password, and only Microsoft has access to the layers below that.

Now that we have understood how the layers are accessed and used to separate code, we need to understand how this works practically when the same piece of functionality is modified in more than one layer. The easiest way do to this is to think of the layers as pieces of glass, all exactly of the same size, layered on top of each other.

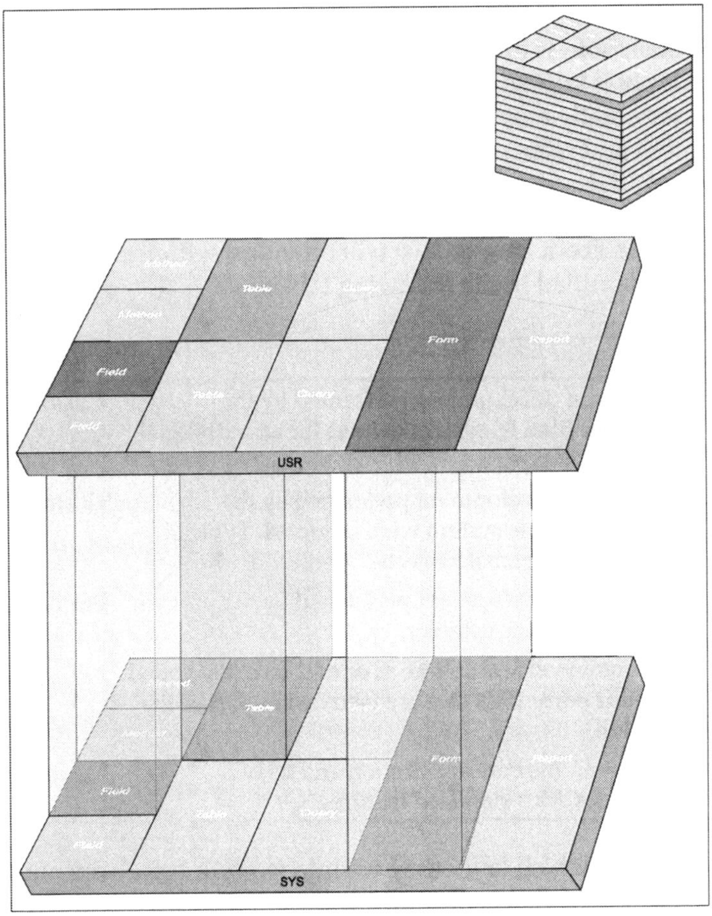

Let's also imagine that the different functions of AX are represented as stickers stuck to the sheets of glass. The bottom layer, that is the SYS layer, is completely covered in stickers because that is where the majority of the standard functionality is stored. When we look at our stack of glass (AX), we are always looking from the top (that is, the highest level) down. If the feature we are using hasn't been changed from how it was originally written, we can see all the way through our layers of glass to the very bottom (that is, the SYS layer), where the functionality was originally defined. Now let's take an example, where the functionality we are looking at was changed by the partner in the VAR layer. In this case, we see the changed functionality as a sticker on the VAR layer piece of glass.

The sticker effectively blocks our view of the functionality in the lower layers so we can only see it as it appears on the VAR layer. If we then changed the same piece of functionality in the USR layer, the sticker would block our view of anything below, effectively overriding the version in the VAR layer and showing us the functionality as it appears in the USR layer.

So by now, we should understand the following:

- The code and data structures that make up the AX application are stored in layers
- There are 16 layers in total—eight main layers plus a patch layer for each main layer
- Passwords tied to the AX license are used to control access to all layers, except the USR and USP layers, which do not require a password
- When functionality is modified in multiple layers, the highest layer always takes precedence

Understanding the impact on upgrades

The reason we need to understand the architecture of AX is so that we can fully appreciate the effect that modifying AX has, particularly during upgrades. The layer system keeps changes segregated from the original application, and allows us to compare the changes made between layers. When we upgrade Dynamics AX with a service pack or a major release, we effectively swap out the lower layers which bring in all the changes that Microsoft has made. The Layers system has kept any changes made in higher layers, and we now have the ability to compare our changes against the upgraded application in the layers below. The developer must decide whether the changes in the higher layer are still necessary and if so, merge them with the upgraded standard functionality to ensure everything continues to work. The use of layers makes the AX upgrade process more reliable and easier to manage when compared to other systems. However, the amount of time and effort, and therefore cost it takes to complete, compare, and merge activities, is highly dependent on:

- The volume of modified application objects in the higher layers (forms, tables, classes, and so on)
- How the objects have been modified (creating new methods and fields has less impact than modifying existing ones)
- Whether the upgrade affects objects that are modified in higher layers
- The scope of the original modification—was it a small change to standard functionality or did it fundamentally alter or replace it

When deciding which developments identified during your Gap Fit you should include in the development plan, it is vitally important to remember that every standard object you modify will increase the time, complexity, and cost of upgrading. It is all too easy to forget about future upgrades when implementing your first version, but to do so is to forget one of the Microsoft Dynamics Solutions key selling points—longevity. Dynamics AX could very well be the last system a company ever buys given that its annual maintenance fee provides ongoing version upgrades. If you stay current with upgrades, you may never have to change your ERP system again. However, excessive modifications to the standard product that result in high professional services costs for upgrades is the number one reason for customers opting not to upgrade.

Deciding what to change

Now that we have understood the power of AX's development environment and how the layer architecture helps us to keep code changes separated and managed, it is easy to conclude that AX was designed to be changed. This is the correct conclusion, unlike many other ERP systems; AX was designed from day one with change and adaptation in mind. However, just because you can change AX, doesn't mean you should. We've already learnt that every change to the standard system carries an upgrade cost, and that the cost increases with the complexity, size, design, and implementation of the change. Keeping all this in mind, it's now time to make decisions about what changes you will make.

As stated throughout this book, the decision to make development level modifications to AX should be made on the strength of a clear business case. Some of these cases are easy to put together, for example, when a modification is required to fill a fundamental gap in AX functionality, or when you need to capture additional information specific to a line of business or industry. The harder ones are the cosmetic changes or those aimed at changing the way standard AX works, because it is not aligned with the business process. When implementing software less flexible than AX, this tends to be less of a problem, the cost and effort required to make the change is usually enough to deter people and encourage them to adapt their business process to be more in line with standard functionality. However, those implementing AX, especially those who understand how flexible it can be, are often tempted to make wide reaching and often fundamental changes to the core product in an attempt to "make it work the way they do". Embarking on this route without fully exploring the possibility of reengineering business processes to align with the standard software is often a major cause of projects running over time and over budget, as well as creating major issues for future upgrades. The following are some key questions to ask when considering changes to AX:

- Will the change fundamentally alter the behavior of AX? As a rule, fundamental changes indicate that not enough thought about how the requirement can be accommodated using standard software has gone into the solution design.
- What is the impact of making or not making the change?
    - **Financial**: Will not making the change directly cost the business money? Will making the change directly save or generate money outweighing the cost of development, testing, maintenance and upgrade?
    - **Operational**: In not making the change, will productivity be adversely affected? Will making the change make a major difference to the operational efficiency of the company?
    - **Cultural**: How will the change be perceived by the users? Will not making the change have a negative impact on user's acceptance of AX? Conversely, will making the change significantly improve the AX user experience?
    - **Regression or Progression**: If the change is not made, will AX be any worse than the system being replaced? Will making the change provide a major enhancement over and above standard AX?

After considering these questions, if we find that we still have some developments that will fundamentally alter the standard AX product or that are implemented for purely cosmetic purposes, we will at least have built a solid business case for the development and be fully aware of the costs both now and in the future.

> **"But we've always done it that way..."**
> This is something you're likely to hear a lot in a Dynamics AX project. Users often find it difficult to accept a change in process, and struggle to see how things can be done differently at the conceptual stage. Don't be deterred, apply the challenges and tests to make sure only developments that deliver real value make it into your solution.

Planning the development

Having learnt how and why we should change AX, we must now produce the detailed requirements and design documents required to accurately size, plan, and deliver the development.

As you would expect, there are a number of key Sure Step deliverables in the Design phase. These are aimed at ensuring that the development and configuration of the solution is clearly specified, documented, and understood. We also start to build documents that will be used for training in the Deployment phase.

Functional Design Document (FDD)

The **Functional Design Document** (**FDD**) builds on the FRD and is intended to develop a more detailed description and understanding of the requirements. A good FDD should describe a process or a requirement in sufficient detail that a technical specification can be written from it, which means it must contain details of the data that will be entered, generated, and stored.

Another key function of the FDD to present the documented requirement to the business process owners and have them read, understand, and sign off the document to confirm that it accurately represents their processes and requirements. To meet this objective, it is important that the FDD be written in a non-technical and accessible way so that it can be read and understood by the key users. Striking the right balance between enough detail and an understandable writing style is the key to writing good FDDs. Achieving a good level of understanding and sign off is critical to the successful creation of Technical Design Documents and ultimately, the successful delivery of developments.

Sure Step suggests that we create Functional Design Documents (FDDs) for Fits (that detail configuration) and Gaps, Integration, and Data Migration (which detail modifications) at the beginning of the Design phase. These FDDs should build from the FRD, the Gap Fit, and the integration plan, and should contain detailed requirements for configuration, modification, and data setup necessary to be able to meet the requirements using AX.

In our own projects, we have often decided not to produce an FDD for every Fit, opting to produce them only when the requirement requires very specific or complex configuration. While this approach can save some time, it is important to be aware of and accept the implications of not having an FDD for every Fit, especially in cases where a Fit turns out to be a Gap and ends up requiring a modification.

Technical Design Document (TDD)

The **Technical Design Document** (**TDD**), also referred to as a software specification, is used to specify the details of the development and will be used by the developer in undertaking the modification. The TDD extends the FDD, and adds more specific technical information that will be needed to complete the development including field, table, form, and menu item details. It is rare, unless the client has internal development skills that the TDD will be read and fully understood by the client. Instead, they should focus on approving the content of the FDD, from which the technical specification is derived.

The content of a TDD will vary depending on who it is written by and who it is written for. A very experienced senior developer for example, will require less detail and guidance in TDD than a less experienced junior. Try to decide on the level of detail you will include and be consistent across all your TDDs. Also decide whether you will restate conventions in each TDD or have a separate document that details the design principals and development conventions for the project, for example, naming conventions, prefixes, code commenting policies, and so on.

When a TDD includes the development of complex logic, try to include step-by-step examples that show exactly how the logic is applied and calculated, so that the developer is able to easily understand what it is they are trying to code.

For use in our own projects, we have created a new document template that combines the FDD and TDD into a single document. We generate the same content with the same purpose, but find that authoring, revising, approving, and updating one document is significantly more practical than maintaining them separately. It also reduces the risk of updates being made to the FDD content that are not carried through to the TDD.

When to use a consolidated document

Combining the FDD and TDD can save time and is more practical in certain circumstances. It works best when you have a one-to-one relationship between FDDs and TDDs, and when there is no risk associated with sharing the technical design with everyone involved, for example, it won't slow the approval of the document down.

Process test scenarios

While technically this is only a deliverable in a Sure Step Enterprise project, we often start production of these test scripts at this point in all projects. Although not strictly a Sure Step process, we have found reviewing the FDD/TDD against a process test script can highlight changes to the design that can be made before development begins. This reduces the number of issues that will be identified during UAT thus reducing rework.

Solution Design Document (SDD)

The **Solution Design Document** (**SDD**) draws on all the analysis, fits, gaps, modifications, integrations, and data migrations to define at a high level what the solution will look like. It is not a detailed document to be used by developers or consultants to deliver modifications or configurations, that is the function of the FDDs and TDDs, rather, its purpose is to provide the reader with an overview of the AX solution that will be delivered and how it will be used to meet the business requirements. The Solution Design Document is typically owned and managed by the Solution Architect, although it may include contributions from others. Formally signing off the SDD is often used to signify the customers' acceptance of the solution design, fixing the scope of delivery, and the basis of delivery activities. In writing and maintaining the SDD, the Solution Architect is able to consider the effect each requirement has on the whole, and ensure that standard functionality and/or modifications do not conflict with each other or are planned for use in different ways by different parts of the solution. According to Sure Step, the Solution Design Document is an output of the Design phase; however, in our experience, it is prudent to start it as soon as you start defining the solution. If this happens as early as the Analysis phase, do not be afraid to start the Solution Design Document at that point. As an evolving document, the solution design should be updated until development and configuration in live operation has stopped, thus it should always reflect the solution as it is in use. This is especially important in future phases as it provides a view of how the solution is intended to work, and will save time in investigating and reverse engineering processes and code.

Practical advice for the Development phase

Having learnt a little more about the architecture of Dynamics AX and used that information to influence our solution design, we will conclude this chapter with some practical advice that may be useful during the development processes, based on our own experience implementing AX 2012 and the Sure Step process. We will cover:

- Estimating development timescales
- Creating a development plan
- Organizing development into builds
- Managing environments

The Development phase includes the development of modifications, integrations, and data migration, as well as the configuration of Standard Dynamics AX. As such, there are many deliverables that we can expect from this phase; however, the design and planning of these activities should be completed in the Design phase. This means that the Development phase is more about execution than planning. Investing the effort upfront in design means that the development activities can almost be considered a black box into which specifications are sent and the developed code is returned. Of course, developments cannot be performed in isolation and the impact on the overall solution must be considered at all times. It is the role of the Solution Architect to maintain and manage the solution design and update and adapt it as necessary. Effort invested by the architect in the Design phase will lead to less surprises and changes to the design during the execution of the Development phase. Key deliverables in the Design phase include:

- Finalizing the business process models to align with the use of AX
- Completing system configuration
- Development of Integration and Interface code
- Development of data migration code.
- Development of custom code for requirements (gaps)
- Completing unit and solution testing
- Developing and completing training guides and documentation
- Completing UAT scripts for testing

These are common deliverables for Standard, Rapid, and Enterprise project types; a key difference being that Enterprise projects will often also include completing the set up of all non-production environments, if it has not been completed already. In addition, Enterprise projects will continue the process of Organizational Change Management activities during the Development phase.

Estimating development timescales

Estimating how long individual tasks and phases will take is one of the most challenging parts of project planning. Quite often, we find ourselves using an effort estimate and resourcing level to derive duration. This method works, providing we don't encounter unforeseen problems or issues not accounted for in the effort estimate. If there is one phase of the project most likely to suffer from these unexpected delays, it is Development. It is therefore important to factor in a reasonable contingency, over and above the effort estimate, when planning the delivery of developments, as the process is almost guaranteed to take more elapsed time than the effort estimate. There are also a few common mistakes people make when trying to mitigate risk of development delays, which are well worth keeping in mind while planning your project:

- Adding more resource doesn't necessarily reduce the elapsed time it will take to deliver the code. Put simply, if you have 10 days work for one developer, it doesn't mean 10 developers can complete it in one day. Distributed development needs to be carefully planned and managed by a technical architect or development manager who understands the implications of dividing the workload. Do not be tempted to use the availability of additional resource as your contingency plan.
- Assuming rework will take no time, everyone factors in time for testing, but many fail to allow time for rework. A good rule of thumb is to allow at least 15 percent of the original development effort for rework and post testing bug fixes.
- Monitor progress frequently and adapt based on actual progress. In our most recent projects, we held a dedicated development meeting once a week, in which we reviewed actual development progress against what we expected to get done. This meant all interested parties were aware of any delays experienced in development due to unforeseen problems, and were able to start assessing the impact on other downstream processes, like testing and training, well in advance.

Planning for AX 2012

Remember that AX 2012 is quite different to the previous versions of AX. Developments that took minutes in AX 2009, for example, setting the value of a dimension programmatically, can take considerably longer in AX 2012. Make sure that the estimates are done based on a working knowledge of AX 2012 and not experience of prior versions.

Organizing developments into builds

If your project contains a significant number of developments or if those developments are required in order for you to be able to configure and test the application, you may wish to consider grouping them into builds rather than completing and delivering them individually. This is a fairly common approach to take in conventional software development projects, but was not widely used for AX.

Organizing your approved developments into discrete builds have the following benefits from both a technological and project planning perspective:

- A timescale can be planned in total for the build rather than the individual developments. This allows us to track total effort and a total contingency for the build. This gives the development team more room to work, allowing overruns and under-runs in individual developments to cancel each other out in order to meet a build date and target.
- Builds can be released in total to the test environment, reducing the number of overall code moves, which can be a time consuming and laborious process in AX 2012.
- Developments can be grouped into logical functional blocks that when complete, will enable an entire subset of processes to be configured and tested. This is especially useful if you find your project overrunning and you have to move to a phased deployment, as it ensures that whole blocks of functionality are complete rather than a spread of developments from your solution.
- It helps to reduce regression, as modifications to similar areas of the system are best completed in the same build.

Creating a development plan

In previous chapters, we have talked about creating plans, essentially lists, of various project elements or activities, workflows, integrations, and configurations for example. Although the details of developments will have been defined in TDDs, we've found that making a single consolidated list of developments is very useful when planning and executing the Development phase. The key to making the development plan a useful tool is to keep it simple and up-to-date. We've found a spreadsheet, rather than a Word document or Microsoft Project Plan, is the best format for this. We typically include the following information:

- Specification document reference (either the TTD or combined FDD/TDD reference).
- Development name or subject (that is, a brief description of the requirements).
- Software Build—if applicable (discussed earlier in this chapter).
- Owners from both the client and partner side—who are responsible for this development from a specification and delivery perspective. The person actually doing the development tends to be less relevant as this is quite often outsourced.
- Effort estimates, and expected and actual completion dates for the following activities:
    - Specification document (FDD/TDD)
    - Specification sign off
    - Development
    - Unit testing
    - User Acceptance Testing (UAT)
    - Development delivery to LIVE
- Comments/Notes about the current status of the development.

The development plan does not replace the main project plan. Rather, it should be used to provide a breakdown of detail not included in the main plan. It should be used to manage the individual tasks that make up the Development phase. Remember to keep this plan up-to-date and consider reviewing it regularly in a weekly development meeting as suggested earlier. We could instead use the Gap Fit document, but as not all items become developments we find it cumbersome.

Managing environments

Having built up a good understanding of Layers, we now need to look at the new Models functionality introduced in AX 2012. Before Models, developers had to copy whole layers or export **Application Object Tree** (**AOT**) projects to move developments between systems. AOT projects are groups of objects that a developer has changed or created. At first, they appear to be very similar to Models, which also allow developers to group together the things they have changed. The key difference, as detailed below, is in the way individual objects are handled by Models as compared with projects. This is by design, to make moving code between systems easier, especially code from third parties such as ISVs.

> **Create a plan**
>
> The decision as to how and when modifications will be moved between environments will typically be the responsibility of the developers or a technical architect. However, having a clear document plan that details the roles, responsibilities, and procedures early on helps avoid confusion, and can help to reduce delays or rework cause by ad hoc movement of code.

Transferring model stores

In previous versions of AX, it was possible to move whole layers between environments. In the case of third party solutions from ISVs, the problem of moving layers was quite fundamental, as AX only has one of each layer. Let's imagine that we buy two ISV solutions, one that adds functionality for handheld terminals in warehousing and another that adds document scanning and workflow capabilities. Both companies supply an ISV layer, but we can only import one because importing the second replaces the first.

In AX 2012, the introduction of Models and the migration of application code from the file system to the database, has effectively removed the option of moving individual layers. Moving Models, discussed later, is the nearest equivalent. However, AX 2012 does offer us another new option for moving the whole application by exporting and importing a model store.

The movement of an entire model store between environments and systems means that everything included in the application gets moved including its ID, irrelevant of the layer or model it is in. This is sometimes desirable, especially during pre go-live Development phase, when releasing incomplete code to testing environments presents few problems until the final stages of UAT. It does however, cause problems when a developer wants to make a partial release from DEV to LIVE, as they have no option but to move everything contained within the application. This requires the DEV system to be perfectly aligned with LIVE, and for the only differences between those environments be the ones you wish to move. In reality, this is almost never the case, and so it is very rare that model stores are exported after a project has gone LIVE.

Exporting AOT projects

Until AX 2012, the only other option for moving developments or ISV solutions between systems was to use AOT projects. Unlike moving whole layers, an AOT project allows the developer to move only the objects they have selected. In the case of internal customer or partner lead developments aimed at addressing gaps within AX, the AOT project was, and continues to be in most cases, the most practical solution for moving developments post go-live. An AOT project exports all the objects that it contains in their entirety. For example, if we include a table in the project, all the fields that have been added or changed are included. This means that a developer must exercise caution when exporting objects that may have been changed as part of other developments that are not yet ready to be moved. However, this is rarely a big challenge and can be managed through careful planning and prioritization of development work.

Exporting Models

Models are new in AX 2012 and specifically address the limitations of Layers and AOT projects highlighted previously. They do this by providing grouping at a level below the object. In the previous example where two separate developments added a field to the same table, each development would be performed in a different model. This means that when we export the model, only the changes to the object contained within that specific model, that is those pertaining to our development, will be exported, potentially resolving any complex Change Management issues we might have previously faced. In our experience, custom development for a build or a solution tends to take place in a single model; there will most likely be interdependencies between developments, which means they can't be treated as separate units of code, for example: TDD001 adds new fields to several tables and forms that are needed to fill a gap, TDD002 specifies a report that includes some of these new fields.

The two developments are linked, and moving a model containing just TDD002, without first having moved TDD001, would fail. In this respect, development in a single mode is little different to developing within a single layer in previous versions.

The real benefit of Models comes when we apply it to our ISV scenario. In this case, each company provides us with a model. Providing the solutions don't modify the same granular elements of an object, for example, fields and methods, then they import and coexist without conflict. With this more granular approach, known as metadata shredding, developers have an incentive to develop more carefully, attempting to abstract their changes in such a way as to leave as small a footprint as possible on the standard object.

The metadata shredding in models dramatically improves the portability of developments between systems, and in particular, reduces the effort involved in using multiple third party add-ons. It is hoped that the introduction of Models will lead to more ISV solutions being developed and released. Greater availability of solutions as well as simplified installation of more than one add-on should also increase adoption of ISV solutions by AX users, as it will now be practical and cost effective to buy in functionality that we wish to add to our solution.

Summary

In this chapter, we have covered, in some detail, the architecture of Dynamics AX so as to better understand the impact of making changes to the application. We have covered the essential tests that should be used to assess the viability of a modification to help avoid unnecessary changes that could impair functionality or increase cost, both during the implementation and in future upgrades. We have covered the key documents that are created in the Design phase and how they are best used, as well as discussing some of the key deliverables for the Development phase. Finally, we covered some practical advice around planning and monitoring development activities, as well as taking a brief look at what the newly introduced Models mean for code moves between environments.

Having agreed the solution design and planned the developments that will deliver the functionality we need, it's time to start looking at how to get information out of AX. The next chapter will discuss the three main outputs from AX—Reports, Document layouts, and Business Intelligence, and how to approach the design, analysis, planning, and delivery within your project.

10

Reports, Document Layouts, and Business Intelligence

The design and specification of Reports, Document Layouts, and Business Intelligence, referred to collectively as system output, could be considered a part of the Design and Development phases and as such, could have been covered in the previous chapter. However, we have found that treating these tasks as a distinct work stream, separate from the main application development and with its own resources and priorities provides better results and markedly increases the amount of Reports and Business Intelligence functions that are completed and available at go-live.

In this chapter, we will examine:

- The three main topics of system output: Reports, Document layouts, and Business Intelligence
- The differences between them in their development and their use
- Where the activities fit within the project processes, and some of the key constraints and prerequisites that are quite often overlooked until they cause a problem
- Reports, Document layouts, and Business Intelligence in the Delivery phase

Finally, we will conclude with some practical advice and tips based on our own experience implementing AX 2012.

The difference between Reports, Document layouts, and Business Intelligence

The terms **Reporting** and **Business Intelligence** (**BI**) are often used interchangeably to cover any information extracted from the system. This can lead to a confusion, when trying to plan what information AX will deliver to your users once it is LIVE. It is a good idea to establish a clear definition of what is meant by each of these terms, so that everyone involved in the project has a clear understanding of what they are asking for and what will be delivered. Following are the definitions we use in our own projects to distinguish between the different activities in this part of the project.

Reports

We use the term **Reports** to refer to any outputs from AX that are run on an ad hoc or scheduled basis to provide a snapshot of information at a point in time. The information can be detailed and verbose, for example, a list of all unvoiced sales order lines, or can provide an aggregated summary like the trial balance. Typically Reports are designed to be printed either on paper or to an electronic format like PDF, although output to Excel for further manipulation is not uncommon.

Reports are typically used as drivers for other processes that are not managed within AX, and are often used for managing people or making decisions. In older, less flexible systems, Reports were often used as an alternative to application development to provide views of information that would ideally have been shown on screen. This is not what Reports in AX should be used for.

Document layouts

Document layouts are often grouped with Reports and are not considered as a distinct type, because they are produced using the same technology. The two key differences between a report and a document layout are how they are run and what they are used for.

The term **Document layouts** should be used to describe the documents that are generated from AX as part of processes, rather than reports, which are generated as needed. Common examples of Document layouts include the delivery note, sales invoice, purchase order, and customer account statement. Some people distinguish between Reports and Documents layouts based on the audience, opting to classify anything that is sent externally as a document layout. While this captures the majority of documents, it does miss some of the other operational documents, such as picking lists, which have more in common with Document layouts than they do with Reports.

Although both Reports and Document layouts are designed and generated in **SQL Server Reporting Services (SSRS)**, introduced in *Chapter 3, Planning the Infrastructure to Support Dynamics AX* and *Chapter 4, Installing the Dynamics AX Environment*, the design and analysis approach can be quite different, and as such we find it best to manage them separately.

Business Intelligence

Business Intelligence, also referred to as **Management Information** (**MI**), best describes the aggregation, display, and analysis of information for management purposes. **Key Performance Indicators** (**KPIs**) are a good example of an output from BI as are the summary lists and graphs displayed in role centers. There is a certain amount of crossover between Reporting and BI, meaning both can be used to provide aggregated information to drive decision making. The following points may help you to decide which term fits best in a given scenario:

- BI is typically provided by OLAP cubes or some other form of scheduled data processing, making BI less suitable than Reports for real-time applications, such as operational decision-making, because Reports can be run on demand.
- Reports can show detailed transactional information, whereas BI is typically used to provide an aggregated, high-level view with the ability to drill down only when investigating anomalies in the data.
- BI will often use some additional information not held at a transactional level within AX, such as targets and thresholds, which can be used to indicate performance through comparison with the actual data. Reports typically run against data held in AX without additional information about targets, leaving the analysis to the user.

Analysing and planning system output

Having established clear definitions of the three terms, we can now analyze and plan our requirements for system output. The analysis, planning, and development activities required to deliver Reporting, Document layouts, and Business Intelligence, fall into the same Sure Step phases as the rest of the solution. However, as these requirements are often overlooked or given a lower priority, we decided to provide a dedicated chapter to highlight the key processes and considerations that should be given to these activities.

Diagnostic phase

The analysis of requirements from Reporting, Document layouts, and BI is an area of the project that can often be overlooked or assigned a low priority in the Diagnostic phase, and doesn't move up the priority list until the Development phase, when users start trying to get information out of AX during **User Acceptance Testing** (**UAT**).

The reason these requirements are often overlooked is that the majority of the emphasis in designing a system is placed on capturing data, ensuring that the necessary fields and tables are in place to hold the data correctly. The assumption is that as long as the information is captured, it can be extracted and reported on later. While this premise is basically true, failure to record and assess the reporting requirements prevents proper allocation of resources to their development, which can compromise the timely delivery of system output. While ensuring information is captured and stored in the right way is the highest priority during the Diagnostic and Design phases, it is important to ensure that the requirements for getting information out are given adequate consideration.

Requirements from system output will start to emerge as soon as you start analysis activities. Lack of suitable reports is one of the most common complaints users will typically have about their current systems, and it is an area they will focus on in requirements gathering workshops. As mentioned earlier, reports are often used to compensate for functional gaps in the application, and you will find that a significant proportion of the new or amended reports the users require are aimed at bridging these functional gaps.

It is at this point that the most common mistake in planning reports is made, that of dismissing the user's requirements for reporting on the basis that what they actually need is application functionality. While the solution might be to use standard or customized AX rather than a report, it is still important to capture the users' requirements and explain that it will not be delivered as a report, but through screens in AX. The requirement must be added to the Functional Requirements Document (FRD) and considered in the Gap Fit and solution design even if you already know it will be delivered as standard or through customization of list panes, cues, and so on. Documenting the requirements and managing them through the formal Sure Step process has the following benefits:

- Assures users who have contributed to the Diagnostic that their requirements have been understood and included in the solution design
- Helps shape the application configuration, especially when designing role centers and security
- Helps to define demonstration scripts for UAT
- Helps prove to the users that they can perform their business processes without the report they requested, validating the solution design and helping to ensure user buy in

In summary, do not be tempted to disregard requests for reports, which you think are irrelevant or a symptom of deficiencies in the current system without documenting them and stating why they won't be required, or defining how they will be met in the new solution.

In our experience, we have found that the following approach to the analysis of reporting requirements helps to address the problem of users focusing on reporting requirements when you are trying to determine actual business requirements. Quite simply, we separate Reporting, Document layout, and BI requirements' analysis from the main requirements capture activities and place them in a separate work stream. This has the following benefits over trying to analyze functional and reporting requirements together:

- You can assure users that reporting requirements are being captured separately and that they will have an opportunity to contribute to and review the list.
- Separate resources can be assigned, to ensure reporting requirements receive enough attention and that genuine requirements are not overlooked without diverting attention away from the core business requirements.
- Provides a set of independently sourced requirements that can be used to validate the data architecture in the main solution design, ensuring that all the data required on the reports captured in the solution.

Another change to the normal analysis process we make when analyzing Reports, Document layouts, and BI is that we start by asking each department to compile a dossier of all existing Reports, including manually created spreadsheets, with annotations and notes that detail:

- Who runs the report, how often, and for what purpose, or in the case of a Document layout, at what point in the processes?
- How report output is generated (print, Excel file, PDF file, and so on)?
- In the case of Document layouts, is pre-printed stationary used?
- In the case of Document layouts that produce multiple copies or carbon sets, where do the copies go?
- What criteria are used to run the report?
- Highlight, wherever possible, information that is calculated and explain the calculation that is used.

Having received these dossiers from each department, the reporting analyst should review each report and meet with users to seek clarification on anything they think is unclear. As a part of this analysis, we recommend that three plans be created; a Reporting plan, a Document layout plan, and a BI plan. Every report provided should be added to one of these three plans with a brief description derived from the annotations and the analysis. Any requirements for new Reports, Document layouts, or BI should also be included in the plans. Just like the integration plan, these plans should include an indication of how the requirement will be met, or a statement explaining why it will not be included in the solution. The reporting plan should be circulated for review and signed off by all key contributors and stakeholders to ensure the requirements and proposed solutions are fully understood and accepted. This activity should be completed as part of the Diagnostic phase to ensure that you enter the Design phase with a detailed and well understood list of requirements.

Stay on brand!

As Document layouts are often sent outside the business, there is usually a requirement to brand them in some way. Consider involving marketing, or whichever department is responsible for maintaining corporate identity at this stage to get their input or guidance on how the branding should be applied. They may even have a branding guide, which can be used during the Design phase.

Design phase

The design processes for system output can be slightly different to the normal functional and technical design document process we use for modifications and developments, because we can use the sample reports collected during the Diagnostic in combination with the signed off plans, in place of our Functional Design Document. We will still need to produce some Technical Design Documents and add content to the solution design, but these are fairly light when compared to those created for modifications to the application.

The design approach will change based on the type of information output you are dealing with. While it is not the role of this book to provide technical guidance on how to create reports, the following sections will provide some practical advice on how to approach the design process for Document layouts, Reports, and BI.

Document layouts

On the surface, Document layouts appear to be the simplest of reports, often containing less information than listing reports aimed at providing management information. Also, the majority of Document layouts already exist in AX as a standard document, and so the work is limited to adding missing fields and changing the layout. Although this might sound trivial, it can be a very complicated and time consuming process, especially if the information you wish to include isn't already in the report document's data set.

In our experience, it is best to divide the design process for Document layouts into two parts: graphic design and data. The graphic design phase should consider how the documents will look and how the branding will be applied. This is best done once and then applied to all the Document layouts required. While each document layout will differ slightly because of the information they contain, a single design style should be applicable to all of them. In our most recent projects, we have used a graphic designer to define the design style and create a mock-up of each document layout required. We then released these mock-ups to the key users to sign off before we started building them, which dramatically reduced the amount of post go-live tweaking we had to do. We also acquired a second sign off of the actual report output from AX after implementation before they were put into production use. Another consideration during the graphic design is where the branding will sit, either in the layout generated by AX or on pre printed stationary. There is no right or wrong answer to this question, but the following points might help to inform the debate:

- Will the documents always be printed or will they be sent electronically? If you plan to send some documents as a PDF, the branding will need to be applied in AX, otherwise the electronic outputs will be unbranded.

- Does the branding contain a lot of color and will the documents need to be printed? If so, it is probably cheaper to use pre printed stationary, rather than printing the document using a color printer.
- Are there multiple brands and subbrands that require holding lots of pre printed stock? If so, applying the branding in AX might be more practical.

It is important to settle the branding debate early in the design process, as it will influence both the graphic and functional design of the Document layouts. For example, if you have to work with multiple types of pre printed stationary, you may need to modify or configure standard AX to be able to target different printer trays based on a field in the databases, such as customer group.

When addressing the data element of a document layout, a good starting point is to output a sample of the standard report from AX (if available), and then list the changes that will need to be made. Most of the changes tend to be cosmetic, that is, remove this field, add that field, and so on. However, it is important to understand what the user is asking for and make sure it fits the document's purpose. For example, many customers want to make changes to the customer account statement, sometimes changing the way in which it runs and the data it displays. It is during the Design phase, when looking at the standard reports, that the amount of work required to make seemingly small changes becomes apparent, and for this reason, it is important to validate the technical feasibility of your designs before issuing the mock-ups to users for approval and committing to potentially very long and complicated developments.

Reports

The design approach for Reports is somewhat simpler than for Document layouts, mainly because the design needs to be functional rather than aligned to any brand. Copying the design style used by the standard AX reports is usually sufficient and helps maintain a consistent look and feel across custom and standard reports.

In terms of data design, consideration needs to be given to how the report will be run, with what criteria and to what output medium. A Technical Design Document for a report should be limited to detailing the tables from which the data will be retrieved, with information about how they will be joined and selected. Details of any complex calculations or aggregations should also be included.

It is at this point that validation of the solution design occurs as the reporting analyst looks for all the required fields in the AX data structure. In our experience, it is not uncommon for the analysis and specification of Reports to highlight fields that have been missed from the core solution design, and it serves as a very useful double check.

Business Intelligence

Document layouts and Reporting are almost always delivered using the tools provided within AX. In previous versions, add-on products were used to improve the formatting and delivery of Reports and Document layouts from AX, but with the complete integration of SSRS in AX 2012, this requirement has largely passed. By contrast, BI is an area where the use of third party products is very common, as the standard capabilities of AX are more of a framework and collection of tools rather than a turnkey solution. The decision to use a third party BI product may have been made upfront and if so, all your design and planning should be based around that tool. If not, the Design phase is a good time to consider the options presented by third party solutions, testing them against the requirements you've gathered.

Whether you choose a third party product or decide to stick with the standard capabilities of AX, BI is normally the most difficult to specify in a formal way, because typically the requirements from BI are not fully understood until after go-live. In addition, some of the data structures needed to create measures used in BI will not be fully known until the solution design has been finalized, configured, developed, and tested. This normally limits BI design activities to firming up the list of requirements from BI and starting to add detail about the application areas, data structures, and existing cubes that might be used to meet the requirements. For example, a requirement to provide sales analysis based on some custom fields added to the customer record could extend the standard Sales Cube to incorporate the new fields as additional dimensions.

In our experience, the design and delivery of BI should be an ongoing and evolving process that you should plan to run beyond the go-live date and into the first few months of operation. Time invested in BI after go-live is often more rewarding and thus, we normally limit our pre go-live activities to:

- Validating that the solution design captures all the required data in a suitable structure and format to support BI requirements
- Start to define and document, wherever possible, any KPIs and metrics that are known to be required and validate that the solution design can deliver them
- Ensuring that BI planned for delivery post go-live will not impact users' ability to do their job and if so, either bringing the requirement forward or designing a temporary solution
- Continuously updating the BI plan and specification as the solution design and configuration is finalized

Once the solution is in live use and the majority of teething problems have been resolved, attention will very quickly turn to BI with expectations of improved visibility and analysis of information that the AX project promised to deliver. With a well-researched and revised plan and appropriate resources allocated post go-live, it should be possible to meet these expectations and start to deliver the enhanced information the business requires.

Delivery phase

Having analyzed the requirements and designed the solution, we must implement the Reports and Document layouts required for go-live. This is logically done as part of the Development phase, but it is typically one of the last activities to be scheduled, because it is dependent on a lot of other developments, which need to be completed first, in order for the data structures to be in place. The following sections provide some practical advice for the development of system outputs based on our own experience of AX 2012.

Document layouts

As discussed in the Design phase, making seemingly trivial changes to the standard Document layouts can be extremely challenging. The standard layouts in AX use a data provider, a class built in X++ code, that retrieves the data and writes it to a temporary table for SSRS to use. To add additional fields, you will need to modify this class, which makes it a job for a developer with X++ skills, rather than one who is only familiar with the SSRS design tools in Visual Studio.

If the graphic style you created for the document layout is radically different from the AX standard design, consider starting with a blank design rather than trying to modify and reposition the elements in the original. You continue to use the same SSRS report and data provider, but effectively create a new design and copy over only the fields that you want. This can be much easier than working with the standard designs that contain sections for every possible country and configuration. However, report elements can contain code in the form of expressions that must be maintained for it to work properly. If you do choose to create a new blank design, be sure to copy elements exactly, otherwise you might find that your new design does not behave the same as the original.

We typically prioritize Document layouts over other reports, as they tend to have a more prominent operational role and are higher on UAT test scripts. They are also the outputs that people are most likely to want fully working on day one of go-live, think sales invoice!

Reports

There are two approaches to Report development in Dynamics AX 2012. Both use SSRS to design the layout and presentation of the data, but the method by which it is selected can differ. Simple reports, for example a customer or supplier list, can be built from a query defined in the AOT. The query dictates which fields from which tables should be included and how the tables will be joined. Criteria can be set, requested, or enforced using ranges in the query, and AX will automatically generate a report selection dialog box for you when the menu item is clicked. This method is suitable for any report that acts on simple data structures and does not require complex aggregation or nested sub-selections of data.

The other alternative is to write a data provider class in X++, similar to the ones used by Document layouts. The data provider allows a lot more control and allows complex selections from subtables as well as a wider range of aggregation functions such as MIN, MAX, and so on. A data provider will also require the creation of temporary tables and the manual definition of a criteria selection dialog, which takes much longer to develop than a report that uses a query. It also requires a developer with X++ skills.

In our experience, it is best to try and determine which Reports will need a data provider and which can be built from queries during the Design phase. This allows you to plan your resourcing correctly in the Development phase ensuring the right skills are available to complete each report.

Business Intelligence

The skill set required for BI development will largely depend on the technologies you have chosen. If you have decided to work with the OLAP cubes delivered with AX or develop your own, you will certainly need a developer with knowledge of **SQL Server Analysis Services (SSAS)**, **Business Intelligence Development Studio, the Microsoft development environment for OLAP cubes (BIDS)**, and the AX data structure. To present the data in role centers or reports, you'll need someone with knowledge of SSRS as well. If you have chosen a third party product, you will need to ensure that the implementer either has a good knowledge of the AX database or provide them with access to a resource that does. The AX data structure is far too complicated to just "feel your way around", and it is vitally important that any custom BI is built using the correct relationships between tables as defined in the application. There are several specialist ISV solutions available in this area, some of which were discussed in *Chapter 2, The Diagnostic*.

Word and Excel Add-ins

New in AX 2012 are two connectors that allow Dynamics AX information to be accessed in these popular Microsoft Office products. The Excel connector even has the ability to write data back to Dynamics AX.

Some demonstrations show how a document even as complicated as the sales invoice can be produced using a simple template and mail-merge type functionality in Word. As Word is a tool almost all users are familiar with, there is a temptation to try and design Document layouts in this familiar tool rather than in SSRS, which may not have been used before. While this is technically possible, it is very ill-advised, as a document, such as the sales invoice, forms a part of the operational process and should be generated and managed completely within the AX process.

The Word connector is most appropriately used for documents that the user generates and may have a requirement to edit before sending, such as a quotation letter. Conversely, producing legal documents, such as a sale invoice, in an editable format might pose compliance issues and is best avoided. Where the ability to edit the output is desired and appropriate, the Word method has several advantages over an SSRS implementation which include:

- Any user with Word skills and security permissions can edit the templates rather than requiring someone with SSRS skills and a copy of Visual Studio.
- The templates can be easily copied to make new versions or brands of an existing document.
- Complex formatting, tables, and graphics are easily embedded using standard Word features.
- Adding data fields is as simple as dragging-and-dropping from a list of available fields and data methods shown in a Word snap-in.
- Making the document accessible in AX does not require any development, they simply have to be added into a library and they become available in document handling against the relevant table.

Both the Word and Excel connectors use AOT queries as a data source. A small amount of setup is required to make a query accessible to the connectors, but once complete, a very simple interface inside Word and Excel allows the user to select the fields and data methods they need. Multiple documents can use the same query.

Although the Add-ins are new in AX 2012 and in their infancy, technologically speaking, we made extensive use of them in our first 2012 project delivering over 50 documents and forms using the Word connector. While it is not an appropriate replacement for documents that are already provisioned in SSRS, it is a very useful and rapid tool for delivering documents that users need to generate which don't specifically map to a structured action in AX.

Summary

In this chapter, we have looked at the analysis, design, and implementation of system output, specifically the subtle differences between the approaches we should take compared to standard configuration and modifications.

The key to successful delivery of information out of AX is to analyze the requirements and start developing a strategy for delivery as early as possible. It is inevitable that priority will be given to more fundamental developments in the Design and Development phase and with a clearly defined scope of work, it is common to find that not enough resource is available to complete the Reporting, Document layouts, and BI in the required timescales. Even if you plan to deliver some Reports and BI post go-live, it is important to be able to assess the impact and manage users' expectations, and for this you will need a clear and accurate plan.

Finally, don't be tempted to start development too early, that is, before all the data structures are complete and tested, as changes to a report's underlying structure can take almost as long as the development first took. Close cooperation between developers is key to ensuring that your Reporting and BI development proceeds smoothly with minimum amount of rework.

In the next chapter, we will be looking at the Deployment Phase, focusing on End User Training and User Acceptance Testing.

11
Deployment Phase

The deployment phase focuses on testing and deploying the system which has been created during the project. Key activities include end user training, user acceptance testing, data migration, and the cutover to the new system. Sure Step also defines that performance testing be conducted for enterprise projects, but we advocate that most projects should conduct some performance testing of high capacity or critical activities in any type of project.

Perhaps more so than in any other phase of the project, careful evaluation of whether we are ready for this phase is required. It is common sense but not common practice to defer entering the deployment phase while outstanding tasks from the previous phases exist, or changes to work already completed are being considered. As deadlines are often imposed rather than agreed upon, our preferred option is to defer some of the unfinished tasks to post go-live activities and focus on deploying what is ready to deploy.

It is also important to note that like the development phase, the deployment phase contains iterative activities, which must be repeated until an agreed level of satisfaction is reached. These include training and retraining users until they are ready to use the system, and user acceptance testing and retesting of processes until all critical issues have been resolved. In a smooth project, perhaps only two rounds of testing will be required (test and retest), however it has been known for many rounds of testing to be required to resolve issues on some projects—even where key user testing occurred during the development phase. As in the development phase, the iterative nature of the activities within this phase can make the exact duration of the phase hard to predict—clearly some slack or contingency should be allowed for. Ideally, all projects would allow for flexible timescales accommodating iterative project processes, but unfortunately companies often force the go-live of systems which are not really ready due to fixed deadlines. Expecting this to be the case, the Project Manager can mitigate the situation somewhat by clearly setting expectations throughout the project. At this time, all the Sure Step groundwork which has been laid till date can be brought to bear in showing the state of readiness of the system and agreeing how to proceed (test plans, functional requirements document, communication plan, statement of work, project plan, fit gap, and so on).

As mentioned here, a common choice is to deploy with known issues to be resolved at a later date. It is even more common to move to live operation without signing off all user acceptance testing. These steps are necessary to meet fixed deadlines, but have obvious and serious impacts on the timescale and effort required to achieving satisfactory system operation. Where these compromises are really unavoidable, the Project Manager's most important role is to clearly record, communicate, and agree the issues and processes that need to be addressed, and plan the mop up of these throughout the operation phase described in a later chapter:

The topics covered in this chapter will be:

- Getting ready to deploy
- End user training and user acceptance testing
- Training best practices
- Testing

Getting ready to deploy

In some projects there may be multiple deployment phases. This is common where there is a multisite, multicountry, or multicompany rollout as well as when phased functionality is being deployed. "Multi" projects require the same stages of project control but will have several nested projects within an overall project and extra tiers of management and communications to allow for this. Some typical examples are shown below.

This first example shows a global project delivered sequentially to three countries with repeating deployment and operation phases (in this project there is a single central design).

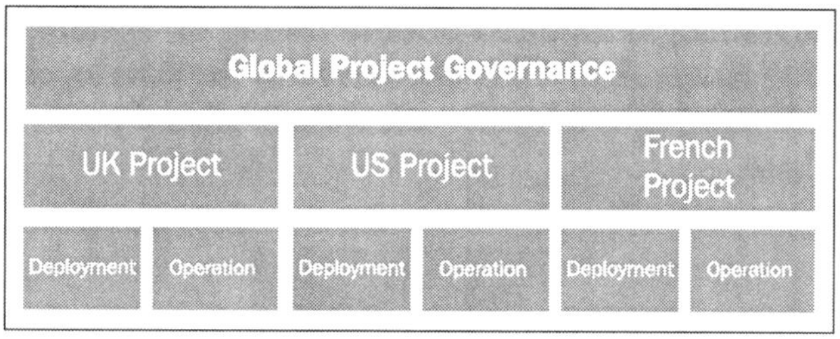

The second example shows a global project where during the diagnostic phase, it was decided to do separate designs for each country. In this case there is typically one or more global designs often called kernels, which are then localized and deployed.

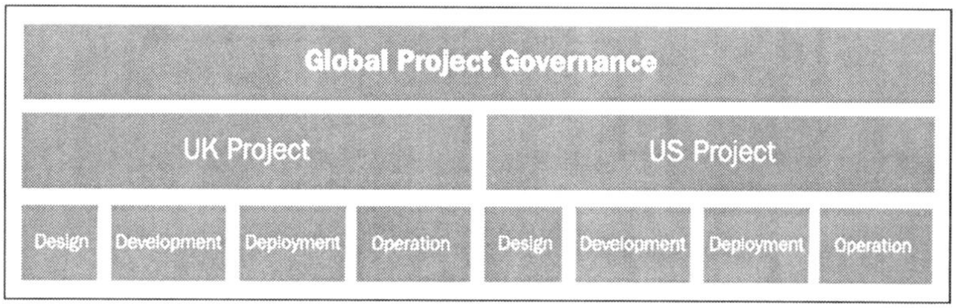

Obviously there are many scenarios which can be considered, the point we are making is that it is important to structure our project, communicate that structure clearly, and then work within the agreed communications and structure. While this is discussed in the diagnostic chapter we have reiterated it because during deployment it is most likely to split the project into multiple threads.

There is more complexity to "multi" projects but we will not cover it all here. One note we would make, however, is in our experience expanding the project teams to include the whole project, rather than just the central team and maintaining the marketing of the project is extremely important.

End user training and user acceptance testing

We have shown, next, a typical flow chart for activities required during the deployment phase. As demonstrated, the standard Sure Step process defines that end user training is required prior to user acceptance testing. It is of course obvious that for users, some training is required prior to testing the system. Key user training, testing, and resolving issues should have occurred in the development phase, prior to rolling out the full training and testing schedule to all end users, which occurs in this deployment phase.

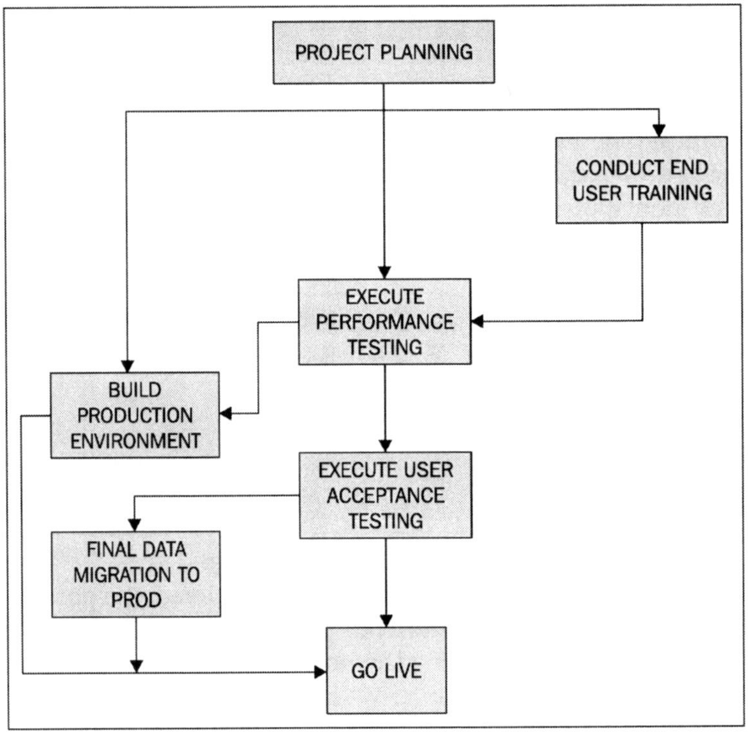

Some projects allow the key users to undertake all of the testing and then rollout the "tested" product to the end users who never get to "user acceptance test" the software until it is in live use. This is poor practice, but not uncommon and the Project Manager needs to advise the stakeholders of the risks of poor system adoption if such a choice is made, and to clearly document such a decision. The recommended approach, as outlined previously, is to train end users comprehensively, and then move on to user acceptance testing.

Security

The most successful outcome can be achieved—for the user and the project—by creating a UAT environment that closely matches the go-live security settings. Carrying out UAT without the go-live security in place is a serious mistake, as when the security is deployed users will probably find problems with processes they previously thought were fit for the purpose. This tends to undermine their confidence in the system and create serious adoption difficulties.

Data migration

Data migration refers to moving data from old systems (including manual records) to the new system. Some of this may be by automated transfer, whereas others will be manually entered. Decisions on manual versus automated transfer will depend upon the cost, the impact on staff, the volume of data, and number of transfer repetitions expected to be performed. In any case, the method of transfer and timing should already be documented from as early as the diagnostic phase (scope statement and/or statement of work) and analysis phase (data migration plan). Data migration is one of the cross phase activities in Sure Step and becomes a project in its own right.

By this point in a project data migration should have been trialled and approved. Nevertheless, last minute issues are not uncommon and need to be dealt with. Having a trial migration helps users contextualize processes during their training and testing. Failing that, representative data entered by the project team should be considered an absolute minimum to support the training and testing.

Data migration is generally split into two phases shown as follows:

- **Initial migration of data into production**: Usually carried out a week before go-live to prevent overloading the system during actual go-live
- **Final migration of data into production**: This is carried out just prior to go-live and typically involves migrating data that has been entered after first migration

It is important to remember to lock end users out of the system while this is being performed.

Training

The training plan should have been initialized during the diagnostic or analysis phase and by the deployment phase, many training activities should have already been carried out. The training plan produced at the start of the project should have pre-agreed the level of documentation and formality chosen for the project.

A training environment should exist and the key users, project team, and system administrators should have been trained. End user training is a different issue, as these users have probably been less involved in the project to date and need very role-specific training for the new or changed business processes and of course the system itself. These users are often less enthusiastic about the new system than the project team and key users and so a structured and comfortable approach to their training is essential to avoid adoption difficulties.

Training best practices

Offering a comprehensive and effective training program is an important step in achieving a successful project implementation. There are many different training methods available and using a combination of these will allow you to achieve the best results. Outlined below are some popular training methods, as well as tips and advice on how to get the most out of project training.

Training prerequisites

Before commencing training sessions, it is important that all "to-be" processes have been clearly defined, and test data has been migrated in order to allow users to have real-life scenarios to work with.

Where there is a high degree of organizational change, it is often a good idea to begin with business process sessions so that end users are aware of and have an understanding of new processes within the organization. This can then be the starting point for sessions that gradually focus, specifically, on end users' defined roles.

It is wise to issue an agenda including prerequisites to training attendees, clearly setting their expectations.

Task recorder

AX includes a task recorder which will allow you to record and replay sessions in AX. The task recorder also creates a word document including records of keystrokes and sample screenshots (every time the screen changes). This is excellent for documenting processes in the system and can be used for training and operational guidelines.

Operational guidelines

Task recordings in themselves are rarely adequate for user training and guidance. The task recording can be edited or augmented with appropriate instructions and accompanied by business process diagrams. Business process diagrams and explanations are more necessary where process change is occurring and should form part of the organizational change management strategy (if present). Don't forget to clearly agree who will be creating all of these when defining the scope of a project.

Training materials

Creating customized training materials can be prohibitively expensive, especially for smaller projects; however, producing documents based around the operational process guides is very useful in delivering training, as well as helping users retain what they learn. Creating training exercises and scenarios that build progressively (for example create an order for a customer, ship it, invoice it, and so on) is good practice and can be used to assess user's adoption of the training material.

Computer-based training and video

Where a high volume of repetitive training is required (say 200 users in a call center requiring one day's training) and/or where staff turnover is high; the training materials will be used frequently. Putting extra effort into creating self-training and support material (perhaps using one of the commercial training agencies) can be worthwhile. The simple expedient of video taping training courses is an easy way to create useful material—but is, in our experience, no substitute for classroom training. The obvious candidate for highly prepared training materials is introductory training which should be given to all users as a prerequisite to their role-specific training.

Training feedback and monitoring

An evaluation form and log of attendees and feedback are very useful. It is well documented that users who struggle with adopting new software will often blame the training or the system. Having signed off training feedback forms (preferably including a statement to the effect that the user agrees the product and training are acceptable) can be an invaluable tool for the project manager, who should try not to look too smug when furnishing said evidence!

Post training

Giving users access to a system where they can practice their new found knowledge will help them retain their knowledge. If we can encourage management to schedule or insist on familiarization sessions for users, this will be invaluable to the successful training of users. The familiarization sessions should include the opportunity for the user to try out realistic scenarios on realistic data as many times as required to become familiar and comfortable with their system processes prior to go-live. This has worked well previously scheduling regular sessions with as little as 15 minutes per day.

Evaluating what else is out there

There are many resources available which can be considered when putting the training plan together. Commercial agencies that specialize in AX training are excellent on larger projects requiring formal training. Microsoft's Customer Source and Partner Source provides a range of free training videos, although we find these generic materials are best for supporting classroom training not replacing it. The full training manuals from Microsoft's curriculum training are also available on Customer and Partner Source and they are excellent for training senior users (not so good in end user training though, as they are too heavyweight, except for some specific topics).

There are also training sessions organized by the worldwide AX User Group (`http://www.axug.com/`) and a number of materials available via a browser search (we recommend Bing). If by this point you have not found AXUG, we recommend you take some time to investigate it as we think it is very useful.

Clearly, training can consume a lot of project resources and this is one of the reasons why the training plan should have been outlined at the very start of the project, preferably during the diagnostic phase, and covered in the Statement of Work and Partner Proposal.

Resistance to change can be a significant barrier to training and especially in enterprise projects, organizational change management techniques should be applied as required. In smaller projects, resistance tends to be more obvious and would be dealt with by exception.

Testing

Testing needs to be planned both iteratively (testing and retesting until all critical tests are passed) and as a cascade through one or more tiers of users (typically key users and end users). We also advocate that testing be split into unit testing, build testing and user acceptance testing as well as performance and integration testing. Depending on the project, unit and build testing probably occurred during the development phase.

Unit testing

Unit testing is the testing of software as it is developed, generally on a specification by specification basis or a small group of linked specifications.

Build testing

On larger projects, the totality of software development may be split into discrete builds, normally covering groups of processes. Although software should be tested at a unit level, build testing should cover holistic processes across a set of features being deployed together.

User acceptance testing

User acceptance testing should cover all processes for a discrete phase of the project and will include all of the builds defined for that phase. As such it should have the most robust planning and sign off, for which Sure Step provides excellent content.

The main focus of the deployment phase is, therefore, **user acceptance testing** (**UAT**); the planning of which should occur in previous phases so that expectations and planning can be included in cross-phase project management. The previous phases should include a documented test and quality plan and this would normally include test plans with acceptance criteria. The rigor of testing can include some or all of the following:

- Tests to carry out
- Data to use
- Expected results
- Acceptance criteria

Results should be documented and compared to the test criteria determined in previous phases, and kept for future reference and approval by the customer. Keep in mind that changes may be requested despite the test results passing the existing criteria. As project manager you will need to be ready to initiate change request procedures, and monitor the impact these may have on the project schedule.

Conducting UAT properly is surprisingly time consuming and is a good activity for a project manager to delegate. Although time consuming, this is one of the most important aspects of the project. If we do delegate this activity we should still manage it by tasking our colleague specifically and reviewing the planning, execution, and output of the testing.

When test results are raised, they need to be logged and categorized. Some results merely need a reply (such as, not in scope), while others need resolution. Issues requiring resolution may threaten the timescale of the project and need to be scheduled accordingly; especially whether to deal with them pre or post go-live. Deciding on whether or when to take action on these results may require team meetings to assess their impact on initial scope and on satisfactory deployment. Some out of scope issues may nevertheless need dealing with. Assessing them against the Conditions of Satisfaction and their likely impact should help determine whether and when to resolve them. One way to help categorize them is to give them a workload and an impact assessment and put them into a decision making quadrant.

Go live

It is often, although not always well understood that the go-live has a huge impact on resources within the company. What is less well understood is how much effort is required and for how long prior to the go-live. In go-live preparation we would plan for at *least* the following timescales:

- Rapid project - one month
- Standard project - two months
- Enterprise project - three months

Because the impact on the staff in the business is so high, the resource planning should form part of the project plan and highly loaded resources are likely to need assistance with their normal workload.

We can also expect staff to be impacted with a workload for a similar time post go-live as they iron out issues and adapt to the new system.

The details of planning go-live are often left until the last minute on a project; in fact some people hardly seem to plan it at all. The reality is that the more prepared we are the easier it is likely to be and it is rarely easy at the best of times. A go-live checklist should be initiated early in the project and augmented throughout the project. Sure Step provides a template which is a good high-level checklist. We prefer to maintain a much more detailed checklist. Sometimes, with several thousand entries that are summarized through layers of reporting, to a top-level **Red Amber Green** (**RAG**) report for each area. We have developed an in-house tool for this, which we call AXUS. The AXUS tool enabled us to enter all tasks for the project and assign them to processes, subprocesses, and individuals with an estimated workload and completion percentage. This enabled us to plan workload against resources and measure progress on a capacity planning and time to complete basis.

AXUS included a Facebook style home page showing updates made to tasks of that day (including new assignments). Finally, we had burn down calculation by process, individual, and work stream to measure progress. Various tools are available including some excellent new Windows examples—we are currently evaluating Eylean Tasks for a different project.

Task management is not a tool as such in Sure Step and using the project plan for detailed task management is likely to become unmanageable. A company called Brightworks has created a Share Point toolset for Sure Step including a task management tool. As Sure Step does not include a tool, something needs to be identified and used (most commonly this will be a spreadsheet).

Shown next is an example of the summary sheet of this type of top-level reporting from AXUS:

Day number 40 of 165 (24.24% of project time elapsed, 125 days remain)

Category	Effort	Total Remaining	Recorded Completed	Theoretical Remaining	Variance Completed	
Analysis	399hrs	18.8% / 75hrs	81.2% / 324hrs	75.76% / 302.27hrs	24.24% / 96.73hrs	+227.27hrs (AHEAD)
Business Issue	7hrs	71.43% / 5hrs	28.57% / 2hrs	75.76% / 5.3hrs	24.24% / 1.7hrs	+0.3hrs (AHEAD)
Configuration	728hrs	65.93% / 480hrs	34.07% / 248hrs	75.76% / 551.52hrs	24.24% / 176.48hrs	+71.52hrs (AHEAD)
Data Migration	3hrs	0% / 0hrs	100% / 3hrs	75.76% / 2.27hrs	24.24% / 0.73hrs	+2.27hrs (AHEAD)
Development	2172hrs	100% / 2172hrs	0% / 0hrs	75.76% / 1645.45hrs	24.24% / 526.55hrs	-526.55hrs (BEHIND)
Documentation	1280.75hrs	62.76% / 803.75hrs	37.24% / 477hrs	75.76% / 970.27hrs	24.24% / 310.48hrs	+166.52hrs (AHEAD)
Documents Layout	311hrs	100% / 311hrs	0% / 0hrs	75.76% / 235.61hrs	24.24% / 75.39hrs	-75.39hrs (BEHIND)
Integration	0hrs	-	-	-	-	N/A
Planning	23hrs	69.57% / 16hrs	30.43% / 7hrs	75.76% / 17.42hrs	24.24% / 5.58hrs	+1.42hrs (AHEAD)
Project Management	60hrs	0% / 0hrs	100% / 60hrs	75.76% / 45.45hrs	24.24% / 14.55hrs	+45.45hrs (AHEAD)
Reports	0hrs	-	-	-	-	N/A
Testing	0hrs	-	-	-	-	N/A
Training	224hrs	100% / 224hrs	0% / 0hrs	75.76% / 169.7hrs	24.24% / 54.3hrs	-54.3hrs (BEHIND)
Total	**5207.75hrs**	**78.47% / 4086.75hrs**	**21.53% / 1121hrs**	**75.76% / 3945.27hrs**	**24.24% / 1262.48hrs**	**-141.48hrs (BEHIND)**

As part of the discipline of maintaining a complete list we generally start by populating the list when doing future state business process workshops, and record the information that will be required for a successful go-live—usually by process, subprocess, owner, and due date. By the time we reach the deployment phase this will normally be 90 percent complete.

Resourcing the go-live needs to be planned in advance to ensure that holidays and workload don't compromise the availability of people needed to perform tasks and sign them off during the critical go-live period—often a weekend. Contingency planning and several go/no-go decision points should be considered as you plan the cutover.

At this time it is also necessary to have considered and planned for the operation phase including supporting users (perhaps using "floorwalkers") and providing help desk protocols involving the logging, prioritizing, and processing of issues. Any issues arising during go-live should be documented and reviewed by the project teams in order to identify the cause and plan for actions needed to resolve these—including additional end user training, possible enhancements, and so on.

Production environment

During deployment, the production environment will need to be prepared for go-live. This should include: servers, domains, security, and performance testing. The Sure Step content for this activity is excellent as well as comprehensive and does not need to be repeated here.

Stakeholder communications

During the deployment phase, stakeholders in the business will be looking very closely at the project. Some will be concerned about usage of their resources, some about how well their processes will operate in the new system, and some about how the project has performed compared to the budget and timescale.

It is important to be communicating clear and consistent messags through the communication channels which ought to be documented in the communication plan. The more busy and difficult the deployment phase becomes, the more important it is for the project manager to be communicating clearly. This is one of the reasons that the project manager(s) should not be deeply engaged in project delivery.

Real world example

Our project had a deadline which was always the major constraint - 1,000 consulting days to deliver over a seven month timescale. The system we set up was for a company that quoted some 1,000 jobs per month and had to deliver 30 percent to 40 percent of these following customer acceptance of their quotations.

The lifecycle of a job covered three main phases:

- Request for quote and information gathering
- Design and quotation
- Planning and delivery

The duration of this lifecycle is approximately four months, meaning that projects envisaged in January would be quoted in February and delivered one or two months later. We chose to go-live by starting new projects in DAX and running through existing projects in the old system. This had the disadvantage that we needed to import financial transactions from the old system on an ongoing basis, but had the advantage that our new functionality could be brought on in four stages—which were our software builds:

- Finance
- Request for quote
- Design and quotation
- Planning and delivery

Having planned sequential software builds "chasing" a critical business process it was essential that each build went live in time. There would have been no point entering requests for quotation in January that could not subsequently be planned in February. To mitigate this risk the initial build required that a minimum functionality from each phase was ready to be proven.

Approaching go-live it was clear that something had to give. Firstly, we deferred some nonessential functionality and secondly we had to compress user training and acceptance into a seven week period.

The biggest compromise we had to make was when one department would not sign off their UAT. Their software build was acceptable, but had some minor issues which were unsettling the end users and needed resolving. We compromised in that they would not sign the UAT as passed, but agreed that they could see no reason why it would not work in the future upon resolution of issues identified. On reflection our UAT scripts lacked the finesse of identifying test results as critical or noncritical. As a project team we had campaigned for extra time to deliver perfect software, but the business needed the software on time and judged that they would rather have the system live and needing further work than wait. We delivered the system and it worked well, although there was extra work to do in the operation phase.

We are not advocating that this as the best practice, but simply demonstrating the pressures and challenges that happen in real projects.

One discipline we found very useful was having a regular (in our case weekly) project team meeting with a formal agenda and minutes. This was run with a dial-in option and proved to be an excellent way to keep everyone in touch with project progress.

We also identified **Project Domain Owners** (**PDOs**) from within the core project team who held weekly meetings with their domains (finance, requests for quote, design, and delivery).

Summary

There are several activity streams occurring during the deployment phase. If the project has been run well, we will benefit massively from leveraging the effort incurred in earlier phases during deployment. Inevitably difficulties will occur, but it is normally difficult to predict these and the importance of clear communication and escalation of issues cannot be underestimated.

In the next chapter, we will look at the increasing importance of project governance and quality assurance in AX projects, and the planning and resources that go into achieving this.

12
Project Governance and Quality Assurance

With every new release, the capability of Microsoft Dynamics AX expands. Increasingly, AX is being deployed in large engagements with Enterprise clients. Both Sure Step and Dynamics AX have been engineered to be incredibly scalable, obviously our challenge as project teams and consultants is to grow with the products.

Two emerging disciplines within AX projects, which must now be addressed on a regular basis, are: external review of projects by third parties known as **Project Governance and Delivery Review** (**PGDR**), and formal **Quality Assurance** (**QA**). We believe these to be very important, and there is often a lack of awareness in many project teams of how important these disciplines are becoming. Although these are actually part of Sure Step's Optimization offerings, we have devoted a whole chapter to them here in order to demonstrate their significance.

There are other solution Optimization offerings defined within Sure Step including: Architecture Review, Storage Management, Integration Design Review, Development Workshop, Admin Workshop, Performance Benchmark, Pre go-live Health Check, Monitoring/High Availability, Performance Tuning, Post go-live Workshops, and Upgrade reviews. The need for some of these activities will be driven from the results of Project Governance and Quality Assurance activities. You can learn more about these activities in the Sure Step client.

Although correct governance and QA is important throughout a project, it tends to become a larger focus in hindsight—especially on failing projects. This chapter shows how to prepare for and what to expect in PGDR and QA exercises, which are becoming normal and critical parts of an Enterprise project.

The topics covered in this chapter are:

- Project Governance and Delivery Review
- Quality Assurance

Project Governance and Delivery Review

Formal PGDR is typically performed by third parties, although there is no reason why an internal team cannot carry out the same exercise similar to an internal audit. Sometimes, these third parties may even be consulting firms who have an interest in engaging in the delivery of the project. External parties might include Audit firms, Microsoft Consulting Services, other AX resellers, and independent consultants, and we can expect them to examine our projects rigorously.

Microsoft has included content and guidance within Sure Step for external reviews of projects. It is wise to be aware of what this contains to help us structure a project, such that it is likely to pass external review. It should be noted though that running and preparing a project for external review adds an additional overhead to project management and governance, which should be planned and budgeted. It is also very difficult to reverse engineer into a project, rather it should be considered from the outset and maintained throughout the project.

Microsoft has identified two main governance review points: the Project Lifecycle review (phase-by-phase) and the Project Closure review.

The Project Lifecycle review occurs throughout the project at phase/stage boundaries, whereas the Project Closure review occurs at the end of the project.

Project Lifecycle reviews

In a lifecycle review, we can expect an initial interview by the external consultant, and then to be asked to provide evidence for some of our answers by submitting relevant documents from our project. Sometimes, the consultant will request documents prior to the interview. If the consultant isn't satisfied, we can expect further reviews and engagements to be scheduled. It can be a good idea for a project team to identify the need for, and introduce a PGDR element into a project before someone else does.

Sure Step provides a Project Governance and Delivery Review Description of services for AX, the contents of which are summarized as follows:

Phase-by-phase Assessment Overview

Throughout each of the phases, the Project Governance and Delivery Review team should be present at regular project status meetings to discuss and report on issues, and to recommend the required actions resulting from these. The aim of this activity is to work with the customer to identify and manage issues before they prove problematic to the project's health. Topics to discuss include, but are not limited to:

- Issues Register
- Risk Register
- Change requests
- Estimated completion dates for phase deliverables
- Project phase acceptance and completeness status

Project Major Deliverables Assessment

It is important to ensure that project phase deliverables are completed accurately and accepted in line with the Statement of Work issued to the customer. By constantly reviewing the status of Major Deliverables, the PGDR team can monitor the progress and health of the project. It is important to make available the final accepted (signed off) version of the following deliverables, and to ensure documentation for Change requests related to these are also available for review:

- Business Process Maps
- Functional Requirements Documents
- Technical (Non-Functional) Requirements Documents
- Fit Gap analysis
- Functional Design Documents
- Solution Design Documents

Project Management Assessment review

As part of the Project Governance and Delivery Review, documents related to the overall project management of the implementation will be reviewed. This ensures that the structure and organization of the project is monitored closely, helping to ensure a level of visibility that drives the health and predictability of the project's success. Main areas to focus on include:

- General documentation process, quality, and impact
- Organizational structures

- Scope management
- Business process management
- Change request management

Sure Step also provides a Cobb's Paradox analysis tool which can be used each time a lifecycle review is conducted to summarize the status of the Project Governance.

The Cobb's Paradox analysis summary is shown in the next diagram. Examining the questions which form this analysis, as well as the service delivery guide content, gives a good indication of what needs to be in place to satisfy a reviewer. A good discipline is to run the analysis ourselves at each stage boundary.

Following is a sample of the analysis graphic that Microsoft's evaluation tool produces:

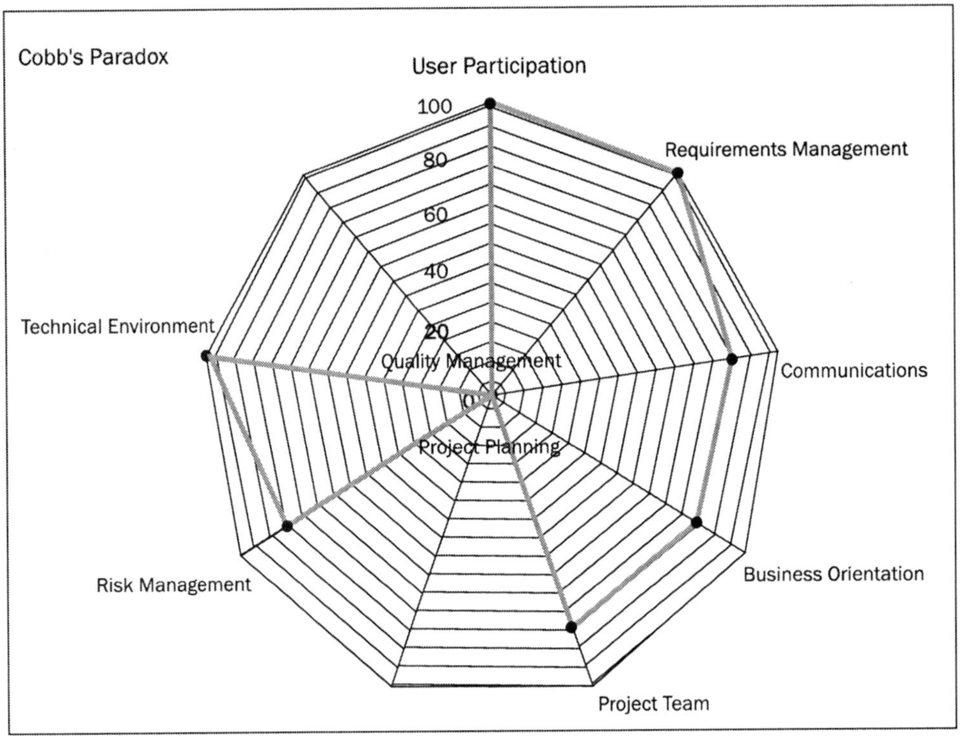

The analysis is generated from nine groups of five questions shown in the tables in the next screenshot. Note that the questions are not equally weighted. The assessment criteria are simple, but far reaching. They require evidencing of the answers to an expert reviewer, who is likely to drill into areas where the answers don't meet with best practices. Where we have made choices that won't satisfy the reviewer; we must be able to explain what was decided and why, and refer to recorded evidence of these decisions. The PGDR is formal and focused, and will not be very tolerant of deliverables overlapping stage boundaries—a situation we have described several times in this book. The key to successful project governance and implementation is evaluating the risks in a project and managing them accordingly.

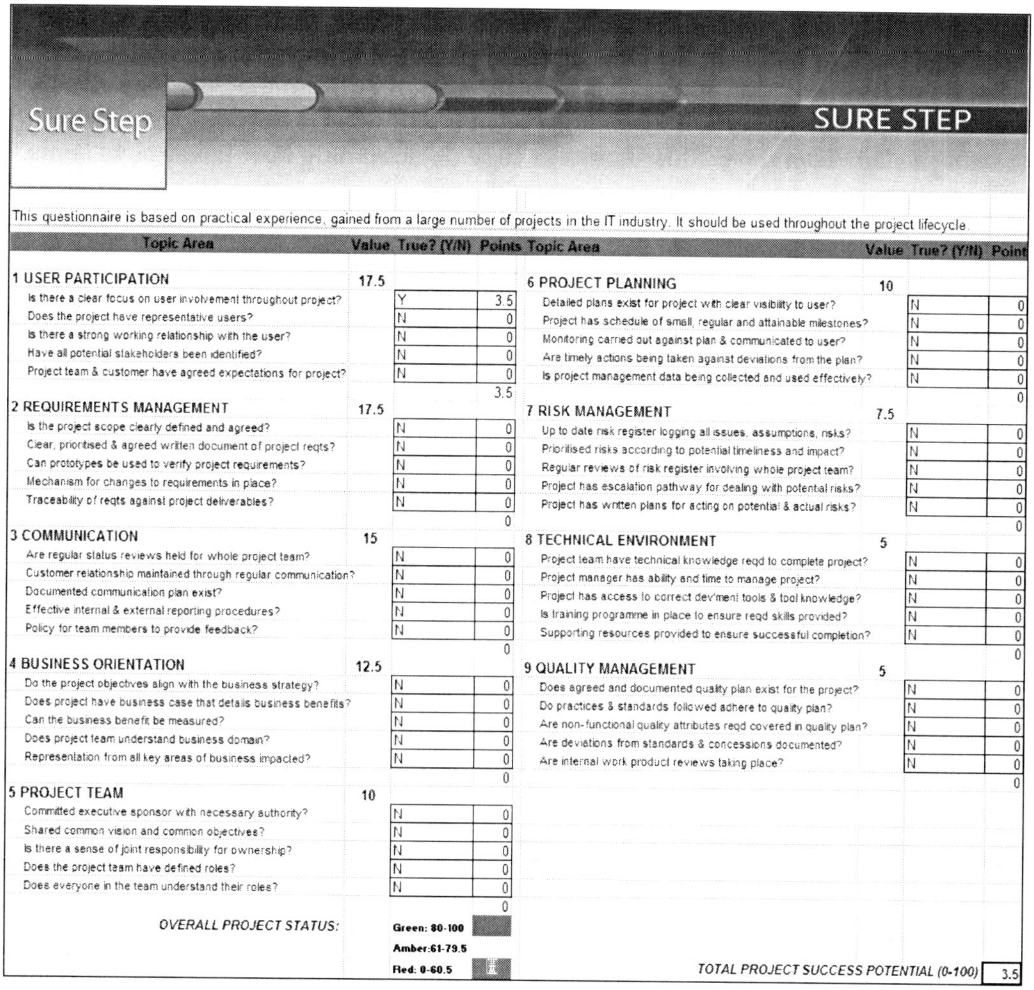

Sure Step

SURE STEP

This questionnaire is based on practical experience, gained from a large number of projects in the IT industry. It should be used throughout the project lifecycle.

Topic Area	Value	True? (Y/N)	Points
1 USER PARTICIPATION	17.5		
Is there a clear focus on user involvement throughout project?		Y	3.5
Does the project have representative users?		N	0
Is there a strong working relationship with the user?		N	0
Have all potential stakeholders been identified?		N	0
Project team & customer have agreed expectations for project?		N	0
			3.5
2 REQUIREMENTS MANAGEMENT	17.5		
Is the project scope clearly defined and agreed?		N	0
Clear, priortised & agreed written document of project reqts?		N	0
Can prototypes be used to verify project requirements?		N	0
Mechanism for changes to requirements in place?		N	0
Traceability of reqts against project deliverables?		N	0
			0
3 COMMUNICATION	15		
Are regular status reviews held for whole project team?		N	0
Customer relationship maintained through regular communication?		N	0
Documented communication plan exist?		N	0
Effective internal & external reporting procedures?		N	0
Policy for team members to provide feedback?		N	0
			0
4 BUSINESS ORIENTATION	12.5		
Do the project objectives align with the business strategy?		N	0
Does project have business case that details business benefits?		N	0
Can the business benefit be measured?		N	0
Does project team understand business domain?		N	0
Representation from all key areas of business impacted?		N	0
			0
5 PROJECT TEAM	10		
Committed executive sponsor with necessary authority?		N	0
Shared common vision and common objectives?		N	0
Is there a sense of joint responsibility for ownership?		N	0
Does the project team have defined roles?		N	0
Does everyone in the team understand their roles?		N	0
			0
6 PROJECT PLANNING	10		
Detailed plans exist for project with clear visibility to user?		N	0
Project has schedule of small, regular and attainable milestones?		N	0
Monitoring carried out against plan & communicated to user?		N	0
Are timely actions being taken against deviations from the plan?		N	0
Is project management data being collected and used effectively?		N	0
			0
7 RISK MANAGEMENT	7.5		
Up to date risk register logging all issues, assumptions, risks?		N	0
Priorilised risks according to potential timeliness and impact?		N	0
Regular reviews of risk register involving whole project team?		N	0
Project has escalation pathway for dealing with potential risks?		N	0
Project has written plans for acting on potential & actual risks?		N	0
			0
8 TECHNICAL ENVIRONMENT	5		
Project team have technical knowledge reqd to complete project?		N	0
Project manager has ability and time to manage project?		N	0
Project has access to correct dev'ment tools & tool knowledge?		N	0
Is training programme in place to ensure reqd skills provided?		N	0
Supporting resources provided to ensure successful completion?		N	0
			0
9 QUALITY MANAGEMENT	5		
Does agreed and documented quality plan exist for the project?		N	0
Do practices & standards followed adhere to quality plan?		N	0
Are non-functional quality attributes reqd covered in quality plan?		N	0
Are deviations from standards & concessions documented?		N	0
Are internal work product reviews taking place?		N	0
			0

OVERALL PROJECT STATUS: **Green: 80-100** **Amber:61-79.5** **Red: 0-60.5**

TOTAL PROJECT SUCCESS POTENTIAL (0-100) 3.5

There are many elements to meeting the criteria above, but we think particular focus should be given to the areas described as follows:

Tiered governance

The scale of AX projects means that regular meetings of the project team are not adequate for governing a project. It is necessary to structure the tiers of reporting in a project and agree their communication methods and frequency in advance. These processes were covered in *Chapter 1, Installing and Setting up Sure Step* and will not be repeated here.

Stage boundaries

The stage boundaries would typically be the Sure Step phases (which we should be familiar with by this point of the book). Within each phase, there may be a need for substages (such as builds in the Development phase). It is important to understand what should occur within stages (this is easily referenced from the Sure Step client), and it is even more important to evaluate what is and what is not complete when crossing a stage boundary. This should include documenting how incomplete items will be managed, as well as their impact on the project.

Formalities in Project Governance

Creating three or more tiers of governance with regular meetings means there can be a lot of meetings to attend and manage. Creating agendas and minutes can be tedious, but it is necessary to provide evidence that governance has been carried out properly and useful in any case for the meeting attendees. We recommend that a minute taker is appointed, allowing the key participants to focus on the content—this is especially the case if the Project Manager chairs the meeting. It is often a good idea to have an effective issue recording tool in place to manage and follow up any issues raised in Project Governance meetings. Something as simple as a spreadsheet can ensure that these issues can be captured, monitored, and resolved more efficiently than having nothing in place.

An example of a high-level project status report has been included as follows to illustrate the key points that should be considered in steering meetings:

PROJECT STATUS REPORT

1. OVERVIEW

Overall status of the **Project**:

RED	AMBER	GREEN

1.1. HIGH LEVEL STATUS REPORT OF KEY AREAS

1.2. DETAILED STATUS REPORT OF KEY AREAS

2. NEW OR OUTSTANDING SCOPE CHANGE REQUESTS

3. KEY ACTIVITY THIS PERIOD

Outline of activities and deliverables achieved this period.

4. NOT ACHIEVED THIS PERIOD

Outline of activities and deliverables that were planned this period but were not achieved.

5. KEY ACTIVITY PLANNED FOR NEXT PERIOD

Outline of activities and deliverables planned for next period.

6. RISKS AND ISSUES

6.1. OUTLINE OF NEW OR OUTSTANDING RISKS

Outline of new or outstanding risks including status, priority and owner

6.2. OUTLINE OF NEW OR OUTSTANDING ISSUES

Outline of new or outstanding issues including status, exposure and owner

7. OUTSTANDING SERVICE DELIVERABLE ACCEPTANCE

8. ANY OTHER BUSINESS

Minimum toolset

Using the Sure Step client, we can easily create a project and see the content recommended for that project type by selecting the project and clicking on the **Project Documents** tab as shown in the following screenshot:

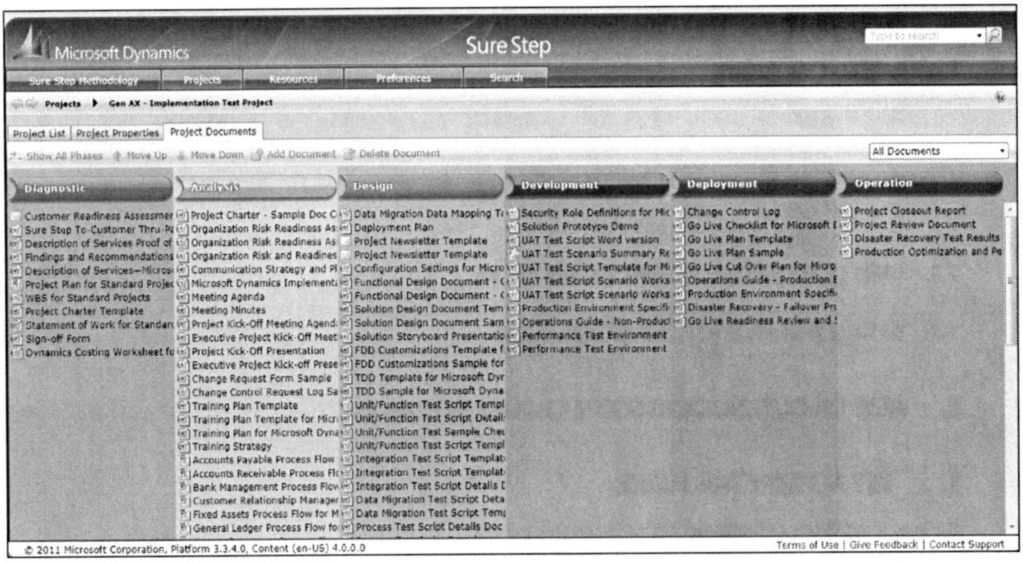

In the version of Sure Step used at the time of writing, there is an issue with the filters, and sometimes you will see that some documents appear to be duplicated. Nevertheless, using this is an easy way to identify the key content required for a project. We prefer to start with an Enterprise project and then delete the documents we don't want, as we believe it creates a more comprehensive result. In any case, our project initiation documentation, including the Communication Plan, Project Charter, Statement of Work, and Scope Statements should clearly agree who develops which of these documents and each of them should also be a milestone on our project plan.

Audit Requirements

PGDR and QA may be performed by the company's auditors. In these cases, PGDR or QA may be a part of the audit or separate engagements. In other cases, the reviews will be carried out by an external consultant. In any case, the audit should have a focus on the security of the AX system as well as the application maintenance lifecycle.

Within AX 2012, security is a significant issue as you will have noticed in earlier chapters. Within Enterprise clients, there is a need to implement robust security configuration processes and audit procedures, and this is especially true where there are regulatory requirements, such as Sarbanes Oxley.

AX has some built in security features, such as the Segregation of Duties functions; however, as a system administrator, access to the system and security is unrestricted and potentially invisible. A company called Fastpath has developed tools and procedures to implement regulatory strength security audit into AX which is overviewed as follows.

Analyzing access, monitoring segregation of duties risks, and target system changes are ongoing challenges for complex, international ERP solutions like Dynamics AX. Fastpath provides comprehensive audit solutions to automate and simplify compliance for Dynamics AX. Their team of Certified Internal Auditors has analyzed the unique challenges presented by Dynamics AX and has developed audit templates, segregation of duties rules and key audit reports that make continuous compliance achievable. For more details, visit `www.gofastpath.com`.

Project Closure Review

Project Closure Review occurs towards the end of the Operation phase. The Lifecycle reviews from the project will be considered and appropriate post-project activities will be planned to address any remedial actions required. Project goals, timelines, budgets, and conditions of satisfaction should also be reviewed to establish how successful the project was. The project team should consider what they did well, what was done badly, and how they will engage the next project, if applicable; this clearly applies more to resellers than most customers. Project Closure is an activity in the Operation phase and will be described in more detail in the next chapter.

Real world example

In our project, a single PGDR exercise was conducted by the company's auditors just before go-live. The audit was passed at the first review, as the project was reasonably well structured and documented. Our Project Governance followed a well documented three-tier module with regular formal meetings and the full set of appropriate Sure Step documents. Even though we were running an Agile project, we used governance at a level found in Standard projects. QA was provided by peer review, which was sufficient for the complexity of the project.

Quality Assurance

Historically, peer review was sufficient for quality control purposes, and external review would only normally become an issue after a project had deemed to fail. This is no longer the case for larger or more complex AX projects and the appropriate level of QA needs to be carefully considered.

A defined QA plan should be in place for any project, even if it is only a paragraph in the Project Charter identifying that project team and peer reviews will occur at defined review points. Larger projects will require more detailed QA and documentation. In these cases, a specific QA plan should be written, and it should reference all of the deliverables and controls being used on the project. An Enterprise project will require a defined QA manager, which may be a part-time or full-time role.

Sure Step QA focuses mainly on examining the processes by which deliverables are being enacted, as well as carrying out post go-live checks of the deliverables produced. Sure Step has specific examples regarding Conditions of Satisfaction, which of course will need to be adapted to individual projects, and documented and reviewed regularly to ensure they are being met. Sure Step also provides the Quality Management Plan and post go-live deliverables, such as the AX Health Check, Performance Tuning, and Post Go-Live support.

It is recommended that a formal procedure is set up detailing the QA processes; this will not only increase confidence within the project team, but will also provide useful documentation during the project lifecycle. Some of the QA activities recommended by Sure Step are outlined below; however the frequency and complexity of these should be adapted to suit the requirements of the individual project:

- Frequent project quality reviews, that consist of monitoring go-live status, possibly including infrastructure, the training plan, the testing plan, security and optimization potential
- Auditing of troubled projects
- Post go-live reviews

In addition to Sure Step's process-focused QA, we like to consider a risk-based approach on a project and provide specific QA in relation to the degree of risk an activity may have on the health of the project. For example, if your project has 200 days of Development and only 20 days of Data Migration, the QA processes required to ensure deliverables in the Development phase are of sound quality would need to be more intensive than that of Data Migration QA.

Effective QA of both processes and deliverables will help to identify areas of the project that are in need of attention, as well as ensuring that risks and issues are managed throughout the project lifecycle.

Summary

PGDR and QA are going to be a feature of an increasing number of AX projects as the product continues to grow. These activities require planning from the outset of the project and a considerable amount of resource needs to be dedicated to achieve compliance.

The parties involved in PGDR are likely to be thorough in their review. In this chapter, we have learnt that the Project Manager and Project team need to operate more formally than they may have in the past, and be prepared to explain actions and decisions to expert impartial external reviewers.

We discussed the importance of conducting lifecycle reviews at stage boundaries through the project, and a project closure activity should consider the success of the project, outline any carried over actions, and plan for any future phases.

Finally, PGDR and QA should be seen as an opportunity both to excel in a project and to demonstrate that we have excelled. Project budgets and timescale need to accommodate these activities, or well documented decisions should say who decided otherwise and why.

In the next chapter, we will look at the Operation phase and the key activities that take place, including project planning, transition of solution to support, and discussing any future phases.

13

Operation Phase

Hopefully the most exciting part of the project, the Operation phase covers the period where the customer starts to use the system up to the point where the Project team is able to disengage and hand over the system to the ongoing support team. The two main activities within the Operation phase for a Sure Step project type of Standard are Project Planning and Transition Solution to Support.

The topics covered in this chapter include:

- Project Planning
- Transitioning the Solution to Support
- Future phases

Activities within the Operation phase

The following diagram illustrates the activities that take place during the Operation phase:

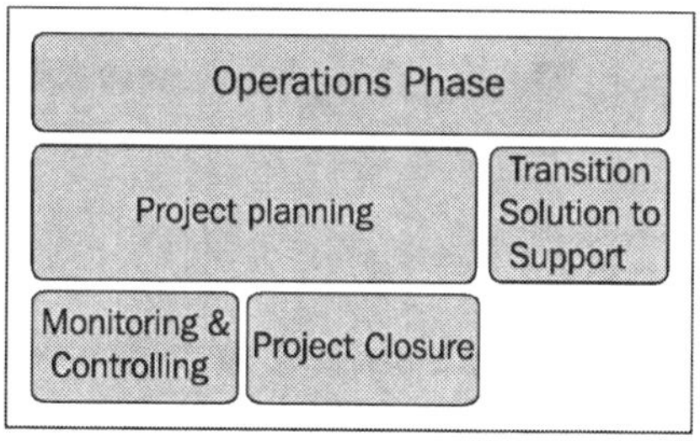

Project Planning

The Project Planning activity focuses on running down the project, and includes the completion of all project documentation, coordinating outstanding project issues, measurement of the success of the project, and communications with stakeholders. During the running down period, the Project team should be focused on closing issues and disengaging cleanly from the project.

As some issues can run on for long periods and it is typical during the project to have deferred some functionality or added new scope to be provided in later phases, it is more common to hand over some outstanding issues from the Project team to the support team rather than resolve every single issue beforehand. The Project team needs to identify everything that needs closing, and then close it or prepare it for handover.

To achieve rundown, there needs to be one or more clearly defined transition points, which are clearly documented to ensure that there is no confusion over scope delivery, timescale adherence, cost management, or other contractual issues.

As usual, the Sure Step Client provides some well-structured documentation and activities for the Operation phase Project Planning. Sure Step splits **Project Planning** into **Monitoring & Controlling** and **Project Closure**.

Project Planning – Monitoring & Controlling

The Project Planning activities are Cross Phase activities and will have been ongoing throughout the project. In this phase, they need to be completed and if necessary, transitioned to future phases or the ongoing support of the solution.

Risk Management

Any outstanding issues in the Risk Register should be closed or transferred to the next phase or ongoing support. During this phase, new risks may of course still be added to the Risk Register.

Scope Management

At this time, all Scope Change requests should be reviewed and enacted as necessary. Again, open Change requests may be moved to a future activity, in which case they can be closed in this set of reporting. Scope Change Requests are reasonably likely to occur during initial operation and new requests may be raised. Most often, these will arise from the support/issue log as described in the next section. Scope Change can of course include reducing scope, where UAT or live operation deems processes to be unnecessary.

Issue Management

During the project, there is typically an issue log maintained specifically for the project. This is used to close out issues and transfer live issues to ongoing support. At some point (usually go-live, perhaps UAT), support requirements will start to be logged in the company's usual support system. This will probably include support, which is not directly related to our project; so one or more members of the Project team need to review the support issues being raised at least daily.

Timescale Management

Even at this late point in the project lifecycle, the project plan should be kept up to date. One or more new plans will be required for future phases as the live plan should come to a close. Once closed, the plan can be compared to baselines set throughout the project and a report made on project timescales.

Cost Management

The budget management should be a well-established discipline by now, and at the completion point, over or under spend will need to be identified. Budget that is transferred to future projects should be clearly documented. It is also important to try and separate project costs from support costs. A good WBS-based reporting mechanism should cater for this. The initial and revised Purchase Orders, Contract, and Statement of Work should be reviewed to check for any contractual cost issues that may need resolving (retentions, staged payments, fixed price agreements, and so on).

Resource Management

At this point, the Project team members are likely to be looking at their future roles. It is important to keep them focused until they disengage, and perhaps prepare them for transition to new roles. The top-end consultants in particular, will be lining up their next engagements, but may be needed if the Operation phase is not going smoothly. This should be a mitigated risk on every project. Having a contingency budget and an arrangement with the critical resources is essential.

End users may have assumed new or changed roles and responsibilities. Their adoption of the processes and system need to be evaluated, and issues should be raised and managed properly.

Communication Management

The frequency of the various project meetings needs to be reviewed and reduced as is appropriate to the success of the go-live. It is likely that a daily and/or a weekly project meeting is required for a period. A good practice is standing meetings just before the start of the day—this not only keeps everybody up to date, but also tends to speed up the process as nobody gets too comfortable.

Quality Management

Quality Management closeout activities and sign offs should be conducted as defined in the Project Charter and Quality Plan. This generally involves getting final versions of documents signed off.

Project Planning – Project Closure

Sure Step provides what we consider to be a particularly good Project closure report for larger projects. There is also further supporting material. The Project closure report includes the following self-explanatory sections and some guidelines on how to populate them:

- Project closure report summary
- Delivery of vision
- Changes that impacted the vision
    - Changes in business/organization
    - Changes in vision
    - Changes in team
    - Changes in customer process
    - Changes in project process
    - Changes in plans
    - Changes in specifications
    - Changes in timelines
- Next Steps: Vision of continuing project efforts, Next version

Outstanding items

A clear list of outstanding items needs to be maintained and reviewed daily, so the Project Manager can check progress on closing the project and that the correct resources and prioritization are brought to bear where necessary. The method of making changes (configuration and development) is different after the Operational phase starts. Downtime is now a critical issue, so server restarts due to configuration changes or code import have to be carefully planned, as does their effect on usage data.

Additional training

During operation, it is normal to find that some users or teams need additional training. The user feedback meetings described in *Chapter 11, Deployment Phase* should help identify any such needs in combination with a review of the support log. It can be helpful to publish short reference guides and FAQs in addition to the Operation guidelines.

Additional training may be necessary for users wherever there has been a large gap between their initial training and go-live. Also, we have found that if resources allow, arranging follow up or refresher training can enable new users to become competent and expert users much more quickly.

Popular follow-up sessions include advanced features, Q&A, tips and tricks, and application shortcuts. It is surprising how much may not sink in during the initial training sessions, with some users being happy just to be able to perform their basic tasks. Even though the new system may provide some quick wins, most users could benefit from regular follow-up sessions with the senior consultants and/or key users.

Documentation

Any open documentation (including the Communication Plan) should be completed and closed.

Lessons Learned

A Lessons Learned session is a valuable exercise even for a Project team that is not going to work together. To achieve anything, these sessions should not be finger pointing exercises; rather they should be a learning environment for all concerned and help structure future phases.

Tollgate Review

A final review will be required to look at the status of deliverables and the output of the Operation phase. Whatever task management tool is in place, it is important to review every outstanding task and close it or move it into a future phase or to the support helpdesk.

Celebrate

Sure Step suggests we should celebrate at this point. If all is well, who can argue with that?

Transition Solution to Support

Once live, the solution needs to be transferred from ownership of the Project team to ownership of the support team. Typically, this will occur over the first few weeks.

Go-live support

During the first few days of go-live, it is hard to estimate how much support will be required. Some of our tips include:

- On larger projects, position some Project team members within user departments proactively engaging users
- On smaller projects, have one or more "floorwalkers" proactively engaging users
- Provide tiered support—save the expert consultants from being inundated with minor niggles
- Make sure the company helpdesk knows what is coming and how to prioritize and treat AX support issues
- Have a Plan B for security (a set of more relaxed roles)
- Prepare FAQs from any common support issues
- Clearly communicate any fixes made to all relevant users
- Focus on critical or high load processes
- Have alternate work lined up in case your support resources are not required to their full capacity, that is, in cases where there are only minor issues, or low numbers of calls
- In case of a high volume of support issues, it is necessary to be able to categorize them with a priority, and set an expectation with users of how they will be prioritized and dealt with—including a timescale if possible

It is important to have clearly understood support charging and service level agreements with vendors or consultants who may be engaged in supporting the system.

Support and Change Request Management

During this phase, there can be a lot of confusion regarding whether we are dealing with free of charge bug fixing (dependent upon your contract) or chargeable enhancements. Logging of support issues and being able to categorize them as free or chargeable for later review is a wise discipline. Our recommendation is that when the customer team logs an issue, they should not categorize it as a change request or bug. However, when this is logged with the support vendor, they should log it as chargeable or not (with a reason and estimate if it is chargeable), and submit a weekly list of categorization and appropriate estimates to the customer's support manager. The mechanism of this should be clearly documented in the relevant support contract.

Resource Management

As the Project team will be replaced by the Support team, hand over of the system and training of the new team is necessary. Ongoing development of the team should be a focus, as they will likely be able to enhance their responsibilities over time. It is also important to identify critical resources, especially senior consultants leaving the project. We should focus on reducing dependency on these resources as well as keeping open lines of communication.

Ongoing support

By this time, the ongoing support should be established. The first line support should be as close to the End Users as possible (Key Users, Team Leaders, or nominated Subject Matter Experts). Further internal support should be available in house, with formal support agreements in place with Microsoft or the reseller.

Issue and Support Logging

While Project teams sometimes maintain their own support log, we advocate integrating AX support with the company's regular support system. In any case, the importance is to be able to easily identify and review AX support issues, so they can be easily managed by the second line support, which is usually still provided by the Project team or a support vendor.

Support issues should be able to be categorized by severity in relation to the **Service Level Agreements** (**SLA**) in place with the support vendor. Reporting of open issues is required, and this would preferably mirror the escalation levels and timescales in the SLA. It is valuable that the user can see their own issues and updates to progress thereon, and that the customer and partner support teams can access all relevant issues including appropriate summary reports.

A regular scheduled meeting between the customer and support vendor managers should be instigated, as should an overview to any ongoing project steering meetings.

From the support system, issues may be raised for more serious items dealt with outside of the support system—generally for matters requiring stakeholders' attention. These issues may in turn become risks. It is therefore, important to agree before the Design phase is completed about how these risk issues and support will change during the Operation phase. The Project team will usually hand over independent lists and processes to the in-house support teams, who have their own lists and processes.

Operation Validation

It is useful to schedule regular reviews with departments to monitor and get feedback on their concerns, and to maintain positive relations between end users and support. We have found scheduled face-to-face meetings to be very valuable.

Future phases

Having succeeded with the initial scope, there are chances of some organizational change during the project as well as new requirements defined. In addition to these, items not initially regarded as core in a project may become a focus. These may often include Business Intelligence, Workflow, Role Centres, Alerts, Exception Reporting, and so on. It is more desirable that these are dealt with in the initial project, as they leverage the power of AX; nevertheless budget and timescales don't always allow for this.

With AX's new licensing model, every two months a routine will check the client license types purchased by the customer and the client license types in use. This could lead to a significant liability to purchase extra licenses. If you have deployed standard role centres, you will find that they are hungry for the more expensive Enterprise and Functional licenses. We recommend that you compare your license usage and your license purchase early after go-live and seek to adjust your security accordingly.

AX communities and resources online

We have included a short guide to our favourite AX communities and resources that can be found online.

AX user group

The primary user group is AXUG. The link for this group is `www.axug.com`. Started in the US America, this is now a worldwide concern. There are local user groups in many countries and these are worth evaluating. Certainly, AXUG offers a good range of training, special interest groups, opportunities to meet people in the AX community, and opportunities to improve one's knowledge.

LinkedIn

There are many LinkedIn groups focused on Dynamics. Many of these are started by recruiters wishing to build a contact list. We recommend focusing on larger groups (over 1,000 members) where there are also active discussions. The link for LinkedIn is `www.linkedin.com`.

Dynamics World

Although it's commercial and contains substantial advertorial, this website has a wealth of information about add-ons and interesting articles regarding AX. The link for Dynamics World is `www.dynamicsworld.co.uk`.

Mibuso

This is an excellent technical resource used by many consultants as a knowledge sharing forum. We have discussed this earlier in the book but this contains a wealth of resources and the partner should introduce these to the customer. The link for this resource is `www.mibuso.com`.

Microsoft CustomerSource

This is an excellent tool for customers to gain access to unlimited training courses, and self-support knowledge bases included as a benefit of customer service plans. More information about CustomerSource can be found in `http://www.microsoft.com/gulf/dynamics/CustomerSource.aspx`.

Real world example

Our project ran quite similarly to the recommendations we have made earlier. The phased go-live brought about by the customer's project lifecycle meant that usage and support ramped up smoothly. We never had more than 100 open support issues (I have managed projects with over 1,000), and most of these were niggles that were resolved quickly or minor change requests. The go-live would have been much smoother if we had not had to deal with major Organizational Change, an Agile project, and the most demanding timescale we could possibly have scheduled, along with the idiosyncrasies of using a fresh release of AX 2012. What would we have done differently with the same constraints? Very little.

Summary

There is a lot of formality to closing out a project properly; this is not so bad if we have been running correct disciplines throughout. There should be strong planning procedures in place to take into account the management of risks, issues, and scope in order to ensure that any difficulties are well documented and considered. It is also important to keep a firm grip on time, resource, and cost management at this late stage so as to not let the project slip at the final hurdle. The go-live support is hard to plan for, and adequate resources should be scheduled with contingencies to cover lighter or heavier usage than expected. Transitioning the project to the support team requires careful planning and resourcing. This chapter has shown us the importance of planning and monitoring your project, particularly at this late stage.

As we finalize this phase of our project, it is important to reflect on what worked and what did not, the lessons learned and what we might do differently next time.

Index

Symbols

A

B

C

D

K

L

M

N

O

P

Q

R

Thank you for buying
Implementing Microsoft Dynamics AX 2012 with Sure Step 2012

About Packt Publishing

Packt, pronounced 'packed', published its first book "Mastering phpMyAdmin for Effective MySQL Management" in April 2004 and subsequently continued to specialize in publishing highly focused books on specific technologies and solutions.

Our books and publications share the experiences of your fellow IT professionals in adapting and customizing today's systems, applications, and frameworks. Our solution based books give you the knowledge and power to customize the software and technologies you're using to get the job done. Packt books are more specific and less general than the IT books you have seen in the past. Our unique business model allows us to bring you more focused information, giving you more of what you need to know, and less of what you don't.

Packt is a modern, yet unique publishing company, which focuses on producing quality, cutting-edge books for communities of developers, administrators, and newbies alike. For more information, please visit our website: `www.packtpub.com`.

About Packt Enterprise

In 2010, Packt launched two new brands, Packt Enterprise and Packt Open Source, in order to continue its focus on specialization. This book is part of the Packt Enterprise brand, home to books published on enterprise software – software created by major vendors, including (but not limited to) IBM, Microsoft and Oracle, often for use in other corporations. Its titles will offer information relevant to a range of users of this software, including administrators, developers, architects, and end users.

Writing for Packt

We welcome all inquiries from people who are interested in authoring. Book proposals should be sent to author@packtpub.com. If your book idea is still at an early stage and you would like to discuss it first before writing a formal book proposal, contact us; one of our commissioning editors will get in touch with you.

We're not just looking for published authors; if you have strong technical skills but no writing experience, our experienced editors can help you develop a writing career, or simply get some additional reward for your expertise.